A Kid's Guide to Drawing™

How to Draw
Horses
Laura Murawski

The Rosen Publishing Group's
PowerKids Press™
New York

To Karenann, whose depth of love for horses is truly inspirational

Published in 2001 by The Rosen Publishing Group, Inc.
29 East 21st Street, New York, NY 10010

First Edition

Book Design: Kim Sonsky

Illustration Credits: Laura Murawski

Photo Credits: Title page (hand) by Arlan Dean; p. 6 © Fritz Prenzel/Animals Animals; p. 8 © Eastcott/Momatiuk/Animals Animals; p. 10 © Robert Maier/Animals Animals; p. 12 © Leonard Lee Rue III/Animals Animals; p. 14 © Fritz Prenzel/Animals Animals; p. 16 © Robert Maier/Animals Animals; p. 18 © Robert Maier/Animals Animals; p. 20 © Ralph Reinhold/Animals Animals.

Manufactured in the United States of America

CONTENTS

Galloping Off

Learning how to draw horses is interesting and easy! Do you like horses? Have you ever gone horseback riding? In this book you'll learn about eight types of horses. Just follow the directions, step by step, and before you know it, you'll be drawing all eight of them!

Here's the list of supplies you will need for drawing horses:

- A sketch pad
- A number 2 pencil
- A pencil sharpener
- An eraser

To draw horses you will begin by making one <u>oval</u>. Then you will add other shapes, such as <u>circles</u> and <u>curved lines</u>. Ovals, circles, and curved lines are the basic shapes you will use to draw horses.

The first horse you will be drawing is the Przewalski's horse. Many people believe it is the

ancestor of the modern horse. Its mane, or the thick hair on the back of its neck, is short and stands straight up. The first step in drawing the Przewalski's horse is to make an oval. By adding a smaller oval for the head and even smaller circles to begin the legs, you'll be able to draw the Przewalski's horse in six easy steps! Some of the drawing terms might be new to you. In Drawing Terms, a section on page 22 of this book, you can find these words and illustrations to show you what the terms look like. Each drawing ends with your finishing the picture by erasing extra lines that are no longer needed. Each step of the drawing has directions to help you. Also, each new step is shown in color to help guide you.

Use the four Ps while you are drawing horses. These are **Patience**, **Persistence**, Practice, and a Positive **attitude**. Before you start, try to find a quiet, clean, and well-lit space where you can pay attention to your drawing. Have fun, and good luck! Now sharpen your pencils, and let's **giddyap**!

The Przewalski's Horse

The Przewalski's horse is the last **species** of wild horses living today. Only about 150 of these horses still live in North America. They no longer live in the wild. Now they live in zoos around the world. The Przewalski's horse got its name from the Russian explorer who first found it running wild in western Mongolia in 1881. It is believed to be the ancestor of the modern horse, but it is different from the modern horse in many ways. The Przewalski's horse has 66 **chromosomes**. Most horses today have 64 chromosomes. This horse also has a very large head. Its eyes are set high on its head rather than on the sides. It has a thick neck, a very heavy body, and a short mane that grows upright.

1

Draw a <u>beanlike</u> shape for the body of the Przewalski's horse.

2

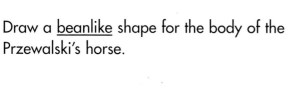

Draw a small <u>oval</u> for the head. Notice how much smaller this oval is, and where it is placed on the page compared to the first shape.

3

Now connect the shapes with two <u>curved lines</u> to draw the neck.

4

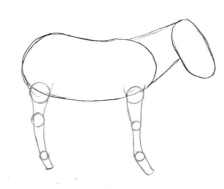

To add one set of front and back legs, draw three <u>circles</u> for each leg. Draw two sets of curved lines as shown to join each set of circles. Connect these lines at the bottom with a line.

5

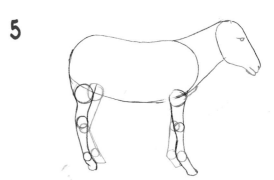

Follow the same steps as in Step 4 for the other legs by drawing circles and connecting them. Draw the jaw, ear, eye, nostril, and mouth as shown.

6

Erase any extra lines. Now draw the basic shapes of the tail and mane. <u>Shade</u> them in by holding your pencil with your index finger on top. Use the side of the pencil point at a slant. Great job! You just drew the Przewalski's horse!

The Mustang

Mustangs are **descended** from the horses brought to North America, especially Mexico, in the sixteenth century by the Spanish **conquistadores**. Native Americans began to take horses away from the Spaniards during raids. Gradually herds of mustangs could be seen running wild in the north. They roamed in large groups across the Great Plains. Ranchers and cowboys, who called these wild horses broncos, started to capture them and train them. Mustangs were **crossbred** with other horses to make strong workhorses for pulling wagons and stagecoaches. Many wild mustangs were killed for pet food up until 1971. That year Congress passed a law to protect the few mustangs that were left in North America.

1

Draw an oval for the body of the mustang.

2

Draw a smaller oval for the head. Notice the size of this smaller oval and that it is placed above and to the left of the first oval.

3

Next, to add the neck, connect the ovals with two straight lines as shown.

4

To make one front and one back leg, draw three circles for each. See their different sizes. Join each circle with two lines. Add hooves.

5

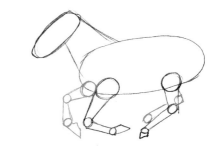

Now follow the same steps for the other legs. Draw circles and then connect them with lines. Remember to add the front hoof.

6

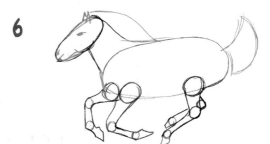

Next, draw the lower jaw, both ears, an eye, a nostril, and the mouth. Add the curved shapes of the tail and mane as shown. Also add the shape for the other back hoof.

7

Erase any extra lines. Shade in the tail and the mane by holding your pencil with your index finger on top. Use the side of the pencil point at a slant and make big, wide strokes. Great job!

The Shire

Most people think that the shire is the most beautiful of all draft horses. Draft horses are heavy horses that pull loads such as wagons and plows. They are bigger and stronger than most other horses. The shire, the world's largest horse, weighs about 2,205 pounds (1,000 kg)! It is a gentle horse. This is why it is often called the Gentle Giant. It gets its name from the English word *shire*, which means county. The main breeding areas of the horse were the English counties of Lincolnshire, Leicestershire, Staffordshire, and Derbyshire, and the Fen country. The shire **breed** came from the Great Horse breed, also called the English Black. Shires were used as war horses during the **Middle Ages**. Today shires can still be seen pulling carts in some English cities.

1

Draw a thick oval for the body of the shire.

2

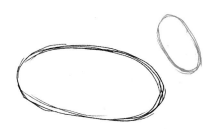

Draw a smaller oval for the head. Notice that it is placed above and to the right of the large oval.

3

To add the neck, connect the ovals with two curved lines.

4

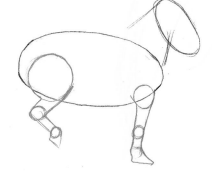

Now form two of the legs by first drawing three circles for each leg. Draw two lines to join the circles. Add shapes for the hooves.

5

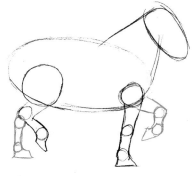

Next, draw the other legs and hooves. First draw circles and then add the lines to connect them.

6

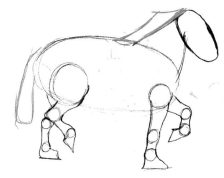

You're doing great! Draw the shapes of the tail and mane as shown.

7

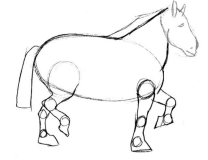

Add detail to the head. Draw the lower jaw, an eye, both ears, a nostril, and the mouth.

8

Erase any extra lines. Shade in the tail, mane, and feet by using the side of the pencil at a slant.

11

The Quarter Horse

The quarter horse is one of the most popular horses in the world. It is part English, part thoroughbred, and part Spanish. In the early 1600s, horses in Virginia that had been brought from England were bred with the horses that had been brought to North America in the 1500s by the Spaniards. The result was the quarter horse, the first breed of horse that is considered native to America. The quarter horse can run a short distance faster than any other breed. American **colonists** often rode this horse in races of about a quarter of a mile (0.4 km). That is how the horse got its name. Later, they were a great help on cattle ranches during roundups. Quarter horses had great "cow sense." This meant that they could guess the movements of cattle before they made them.

1

Draw a beanlike shape for the body of the quarter horse.

2

Add a small oval for the head. Notice how this oval is placed. It is placed a little above and to the right of the first shape.

3

Now connect the two shapes with two curved lines. These lines form the neck.

4

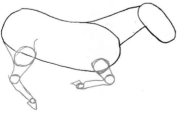

Next, draw three circles for the front leg and three more for the back leg. Draw lines to connect them as shown. Add the hooves.

5

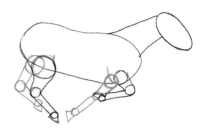

Now form the other legs. Draw circles and then add the lines to connect them. Draw the hooves.

6

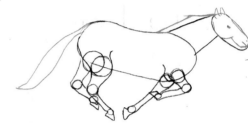

Next, add detail to the head by drawing the lower jaw, both ears, an eye, one nostril, and the mouth. Draw the shapes for the tail and mane as shown.

7

You're almost done! Erase any extra lines. Shade in the tail and the mane by holding the pencil with your index finger. Use the side of the pencil point at a slant by making big, wide strokes.
Great job!

The Thoroughbred

The thoroughbred is the fastest horse in the world. It was first used for racing about 300 years ago in England. The thoroughbred is a crossbreed. It is the result of crossing English mares and three stallions. The stallions are Byerly Turk, Dorley Arabian, and Gondolphin Barb. The thoroughbred is a handsome and lively horse. It has an **elegant** head and neck, a long back and legs, and a broad chest. It is very smart and brave and it has a lot of energy. This makes it an excellent racehorse, polo pony, hunter, and jumper.

One of the most famous thoroughbreds was called Secretariat. Secretariat won the Triple Crown in May 1973. To win the Triple Crown, a horse has to win three different races in the same year. These races are the Kentucky Derby, the Preakness, and the Belmont Stakes.

1

Draw an oval for the body of the thoroughbred. Notice how it is tilted.

2

Draw a smaller oval for the head. This oval is tilted the opposite way from the big oval.

3

Now connect the ovals with two curved lines as shown. This shape forms the neck.

4

To draw the first two legs and hooves, add four circles for each leg. Add two lines to connect the circles. Add the hooves.

5

Follow the same directions as in Step 4 to draw the other legs.

6

Excellent! Next, add some detail to the head by drawing the jaws, both ears, an eye, a nostril, and the mouth. Draw the shapes for the tail and mane as shown.

7

Erase any extra lines. Fill in the tail and the mane by holding your pencil tip on its side. Make big, wide strokes.

The Appaloosa

The Appaloosa's coat has many spots and beautiful splashes of color. The Appaloosa is a very fast, strong, and gentle horse. It is good at jumping and racing over both short and long distances.

The Appaloosa descends from horses brought over to America by the Spanish in the 1500s. The Nez Percé Indians are said to have developed the Appaloosa breed. The Appaloosa got its name from the Palouse River, which flows in northwestern Idaho and southeastern Washington. The Nez Percé rode Appaloosas during their battles with the United States cavalry in the late 1800s. This type of horse was nearly killed off when the troops took the Native Americans' land. Since 1938, the Appaloosa Horse Club has worked to help save this breed from **extinction**.

16

1

Draw an oval for the body of the Appaloosa.

2

Next, draw a smaller oval for the head. Notice how much smaller this oval is, and where it is placed on the page compared to the first oval.

3

Now connect the ovals with two curved lines to draw the neck. Great job!

4

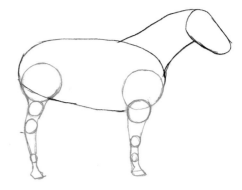

Now for two of the legs, draw four circles for each. Next, add two curved lines to connect the circles. Add the hooves.

5

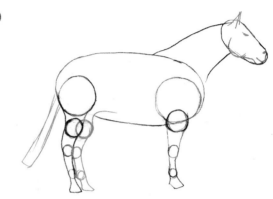

Follow the same steps as in Step 4 to form the other back leg. Draw circles and then add two lines to join them. Add some detail to the head by drawing in the lower jaw, the ears, an eye, and the mouth.

6

Erase any extra lines. Now draw the spots as shown. Add the tail and the mane by using the side of your pencil point at a slant. Great job!

The Arabian

One of the oldest and purest horse breeds is the Arabian. Most people value the Arabian for its beauty, strength, speed, fearlessness, and **intelligence**. The Arabian appears in ancient art. This tells us that it probably lived as long ago as 2000 B.C. The Arabian was raised by bedouins, **nomadic** people of the Arabian, Syrian, and North African deserts. During the seventh century, the Arabian was introduced to other countries when the religion of **Islam** began to spread across North Africa and into Spain. The Arabian is the **forefather** of a few different horse breeds, including the thoroughbred. The Arabian is a great horse for trail riding and racing.

1

Draw an oval for the body of the Arabian.

2

Draw a smaller oval at the upper right of the larger one for the head. Notice how much smaller it is and where it is placed on the page compared to the large oval.

3

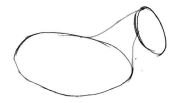

Now to draw the neck, connect the ovals with two curved lines.

4

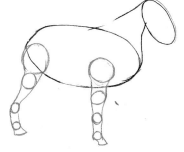

Draw eight circles as shown. Draw four for one front leg and four for one back leg. These circles get smaller as you go down the body. Join each set of circles with two curved lines.

5

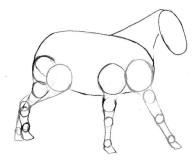

Now draw the same shapes for the other two legs by drawing circles and connecting them with lines as shown.

6

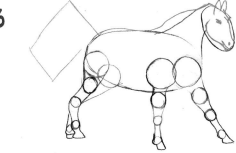

Next, add some detail to the head by drawing the lower jaw, the ears, an eye, a nostril, and the mouth. Now draw the basic shapes of the tail and mane as shown.

7

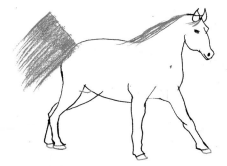

Erase any extra lines. Shade in the tail and the mane by holding the pencil with your index finger and using the side of the pencil point at a slant. Make big, wide strokes. You did it! Great job!

19

The Shetland Pony

The Shetland pony is one of the smallest horses in the world. It is named after the Shetland Islands off the northern coast of Scotland. There have been Shetlands on the islands for hundreds of years. Although the Shetland pony is very small, it is one of the strongest horses for its size. Its combination of size and strength made it very useful for working in the coal mines during the nineteenth century. Its small size also makes it a great pony for young riders. Shetlands are smart and sometimes a little **stubborn**. They had to be strong to survive the hard weather conditions of northern Scotland. Shetlands are kind and gentle and have been known to give great joy and companionship to children.

Draw an oval for the body of the Shetland.

2

Draw a smaller oval for the head. Notice that it is placed above and to the right of the the first oval.

3

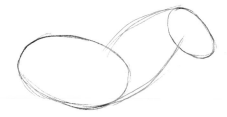

Now connect the ovals with two curved lines to draw the neck.

4

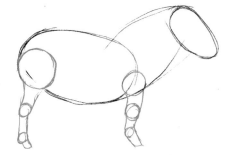

Add two of the legs by first drawing three circles for each leg. Draw two sets of curved lines as shown to join the circles. Add the hooves.

5

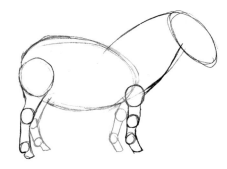

Now follow the same steps in Step 4 for the other legs. Draw the circles first and then add the lines to join them. Add the two hooves.

6

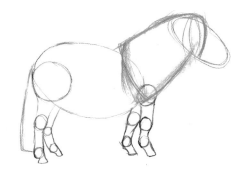

Now draw the shapes of the tail and mane as shown.

7

Erase any extra lines. Add the small, curved line for the mouth. Shade in the tail and the mane by holding your pencil on its side and at a slant. Make big, wide strokes. Well done!

Drawing Terms

These are some of the words and shapes you will need to draw horses:

beanlike shape

circle

curved line

oval

shade

Glossary

ancestor (AN-ses-tur) A relative who lived long ago.

attitude (AH-tih-tood) A person's outlook or position toward a fact or situation.

breed (BREED) A group of animals that look very much alike and have the same kind of relatives.

chromosomes (KROH-muh-sohmz) The parts of a cell that hold genes.

colonists (KAH-luh-nists) People who live in a colony, a place where they are still ruled by the leaders and laws of their old country.

conquistadors (kon-KEES-tuh-dors) Spanish explorers who tried to take over Mexico by force in the 1500s.

crossbred (KROS-bred) When two or more kinds of breeds within the same species are crossed.

descended (dih-SEN-did) Born of a certain family or group.

elegant (EH-lih-gint) Being graceful or beautiful.

extinction (ik-STINKT-shun) Wiping out or bringing something to an end.

forefather (FOR-fa-thur) A relative or a person who lived long ago.

giddyap (gih-dee-ep) A command given to a horse to make it go ahead or go faster.

hooves (HUVZ) The hard coverings on the feet of certain animals.

intelligence (in-TEH-lih-jintz) The ability to learn and to have understanding.

Islam (IS-lem) The religion based on the teachings of Mohammed as they appear in the Koran.

Middle Ages (MID-dul AY-gez) The period in European history between ancient and modern times, from about A.D. 500 to about 1450.

nomadic (noh-MA-dik) A group of people who move from place to place to find food and shelter.

nostril (NOS-trel) One of two openings in the nose.

patience (PAY-shunts) The ability to wait calmly for something.

persistence (per-SIS-tehns) Continuing to do something without giving up.

species (SPEE-sheez) A group of living things that have certain basic things in common.

stubborn (STUH-burn) Wanting to have one's own way or being difficult to deal with.

Index

Web Sites

Due to the changing nature of Internet links, PowerKids Press
has developed an online list of Web sites related to the subject
of this book. This site is updated regularly. Please use this link
to access the list:
www.powerkidslinks.com/kgd/horse/

Why are they leaving one continent for another? What dangers do their journeys pose? How will their travels change the world?

[
What beliefs, hopes, and fears push them forward to new lands, new lives?
]

Every fall, millions of monarch butterflies travel 2,000 miles from southern Canada to the mountains of central Mexico. When the seasons change on the Serengeti Plains of East Africa, wildebeest gallop in massive herds around a 300-mile loop to find water and grass. Humpback whales swim 5,000 miles south in search of warmer waters in which to mate and give birth. What other species migrate? Humans!

Although other species travel, humans are master migrators. Since our origin as a species some 200,000 years ago, humans have been on the march. Human migration refers to the movement of people from one place to another. No other creature has trekked so far or inhabits so many different types of environments. The icy continent of Antarctica is the only place on Earth where humans have not settled permanently.

While animal migration is driven by a biological instinct sparked by a change in hormones or air temperature, humans rely on reason and logic. The rest of the animal kingdom migrates in order to find food, to reproduce, or in response to a change in seasons. But humans move in order to find better lives for themselves and their families.

LOST CONTINENT OF SUNDA

Sea levels were much lower 50,000 years ago, and the islands of Sumatra, Java, and Borneo were joined to the Malay Peninsula. This area formed a land mass connected to Asia called Sunda. Today, much of Sunda is submerged and we are left with only the islands above the surface of the ocean.

TRAVEL TIPS

It used to be said, "The sun never sets on the British Empire." England had colonies on so many continents, including Africa, Asia, and North America, that it was always daylight in at least one of them.

Colonies are usually established by countries that are wealthy and technologically advanced.

TYPES OF HUMAN MIGRATION

There are four main types of human migration. The most common is home-community migration. This is when people move from one place to another within their own community. For example, when you graduate from high school, you might move to another city to attend college or to find a job. It's likely, though, that you will remain in your native country.

A second form of migration is called colonization. This is when a group of people leaves the community to establish towns and cities just like the ones in the country they are leaving. Migrants who colonize transplant their language, laws, and customs into the new land.

When migrants set up their new societies, they often displace the people who were already living there. For example, the United States was founded by people from Great Britain who built colonies along the eastern coast of North America in the seventeenth century. Eventually, conflict between the white colonists and the people they called Indians forced many Native American tribes to migrate westward in order to survive.

Sometimes, an entire society will relocate. This third type of migration, called whole-community migration, is rare today, but it was common during prehistoric times. Just as the herds of wildebeest must move to find food and water, so, too, did ancient hunters and gatherers follow the herds of migratory animals that they depended on for sustenance.

The fourth type of human migration is cross-community migration. This occurs when individuals relocate to different societies. Cross-community migrants might move to seek work. Maybe they are fleeing political or religious persecution or maybe they are just in search of adventure. Some of these migrants intend to settle permanently in new lands. Others might be sojourners who are there for a specific purpose, but intend to return home again.

[Migration changes these individuals and the communities they leave and enter.]

The way a migrant speaks, what he thinks, what he believes, and even what he eats will leave behind a kind of cultural fingerprint. It marks his passage through his new home.

This cultural communication is a two-way street. Migrants also adopt the technology, values, and customs of the host society and communicate these customs back to friends and family in their homeland. Cross-community migration has been a huge force of global change for millennia.

Consider this simple example—pizza. Next time you order a pizza, study a slice before you bite into it. The tomatoes in the sauce are native to the Americas. Migrants brought them back to Europe in the decades after Christopher Columbus's voyages to the Caribbean in the late fifteenth century.

TRAVEL TIPS

Today, some people, such as the Mongolian Kazakhs, still live a semi-nomadic lifestyle, moving as they herd sheep, goats, yaks, camels, and horses from one grazing land to another. They practice whole-community migration.

Pizza itself was invented in Naples, Italy, in the eighteenth century as a fast food for workers in the busy harbor. In the late nineteenth century, Italian immigrants came to the United States for factory jobs and began to replicate their native dish. The pizza caught on and now you can find pizza parlors all over the world.

[Pizza is just one example of how cross-community migration has changed our global diet.]

MIGRATION ISSUES TODAY

If you watch the nightly news on television or read the newspaper, chances are you will encounter a story about migrants. Human traffickers help desperate people sneak across international boundaries. Border guards detain migrants who do not have the correct documentation. National leaders argue about whether it's better to close their doors to immigrants or welcome them with helpful policies.

Debates over migration are linked to how people define their national and racial identities. Today, these discussions often become heated and sometimes even violent. In order to understand these current controversies, we need to examine why humans migrate and what the results of that movement have been throughout history.

Migration has been a driving force in civilization—sometimes for good, sometimes for ill. Humans on the move have spread both democracy and disease. Human migration has led to the birth of some civilizations and the destruction of others. Tens of thousands of years ago, the first humans walked out of Africa. People are still walking today, and will continue to do so in the future.

We all descend from migrants, and most of us will move at some time in our lives. The story of human migration is a shared story—one that belongs to all of us.

The words *migrant*, *immigrant*, and *emigrant* are related, but not the same. *Migrate* means "to move" and a *migrant* refers to a person who moves. Usually people use the phrase *migrant worker* to refer to someone who moves in search of work.

The words *immigrant* and *emigrant* depend on one's geographical perspective. An *immigrant* is a person who has come into a country, while an *emigrant* is someone who has left a country. If you are an American referring to the Brazilian who lives next door to you, that Brazilian neighbor is an immigrant from Brazil. But the Brazilian would call herself an emigrant from Brazil.

KEY QUESTIONS

- How did the continent of Sunda get lost? Are there other continents that have disappeared since the origin of the human species?

- Can instinct drive human migration the way it does for other animal species?

- Of the four types of human migration, which type could you see yourself doing when you get older?

- Which of the four types of human migration most often leads to conflict between people or between nations?

VOCAB LAB

Write down what you think each word means:

migrant, home-community migration, colonization, whole-community migration, cross-community migration, and **human trafficker.**

Compare your definitions with those of your friends or classmates. Did you all come up with the same meanings? Turn to the text and glossary if you need help.

TALKING TRASH

The trash people throw out reveals a lot about human behavior. Prehistoric garbage dumps, called middens, are gold mines of information for archaeologists. Trash can reveal when people from a culture lived, what technology the people used, what the environment was like, and how the people obtained their food. In this activity you will examine a bag of garbage to see what your trash has to say about your community.

Caution: Ask an adult to remove any unsanitary or unsafe garbage in your trash bags.

- **Divide into small groups.** Each group gets a bag of trash. Put on rubber gloves. Remove the trash from the bag and lay it out on the newspaper. Separate the trash into different categories. What are some ways you can classify the garbage? By color? By function? By material? Record your observations.

- **Make logical inferences based on your observations.** When you infer, you make meaning from your observations. Use the example on this page to help organize your work. When archaeologists dig through middens, they want to know the following.

  - Who used these items?

  - What does the trash reveal about the society's religion, government, and educational systems?

  - What technology did the society use?

- **Share your group's inferences with the other groups and listen to their conclusions.** What main conclusion can you all agree on about the society that threw these items away?

To investigate more, combine trash from different locations into one bag. How does this change your classification system? Consider what might be missing from this trash pile. Were items removed for safety or sanitation reasons? What would these additional items reveal about this society? Try putting the trash in chronological order. How does a trash timeline change your understanding of the people who threw these items away?

LEARN FROM A FOOD CARRY-OUT CONTAINER

Observation: One Styrofoam box with attached lid, 6 by 8 by 2 inches. No seams on any side of the box. All sides are of identical dimensions.

Inferences: This culture uses machine manufacturing to mold identical objects. Therefore, speed and standardization are more important to them than artistry. This culture uses plastic and, therefore, either drills for petroleum or trades for it.

Chapter One

Stones, Bones, and DNA

What methods do scientists use when studying the remains and artifacts of prehistoric people?

Scientists follow the scientific method when dating samples and determining what species they originated from.

The story of human migration is an old tale, far older than the written word. Prehistoric people did not leave maps or photographs or diaries to document their travels. Instead, their story lies in fragments of bone bleached white by the sun and in artifacts such as flakes of stone sharp enough to slice skin.

Deciphering the clues hidden in stones, bones, and DNA requires the expertise of specialized scientists. In this chapter, we will explore the methods that paleoanthropologists, archaeologists, and geneticists use to piece together the puzzle of human migration in prehistoric times.

In the movies, people who hunt for the secrets of the past are swashbuckling heroes, such as Indiana Jones. They fight villains with one hand and grab ancient treasure with the other. This romantic image is off the mark. The scientists working to unlock the secrets of prehistoric migration spend as much time in a lab as they do in the field, and they use the scientific method to prove their theories.

PALEOANTHROPOLOGISTS AT WORK

The Afar Basin is in Ethiopia, Africa. This geographical depression sits on top of a rift in the earth's crust where volcanoes and earthquakes have shredded and molded the land for millennia. Scientists study satellite images of this area to identify potential sites where they might find human remains or artifacts. In the 1990s, Tim White, a paleoanthropologist from the University of California at Berkeley, examined a satellite image of an area along the Awash River that runs through the Afar Basin and liked what he saw.

The image showed a blue spot—a lake. The stripe traveling north of the lake was a forest. Much of the rock on the image was bare, indicating desert. However, some of it was white, a sign of sediment. In the Afar Basin, earthquakes and volcanoes cause ancient sediment to rise to the surface. Torrential rains and flash floods spill that sediment across the plain.

[
When the flood water dries up, bones and stones from different eras are exposed.
]

TRAVEL TIPS

Paleoanthropologists can spend days, weeks, months, even years in the field without discovering a human bone.

Satellite view of the area along the Awash River of the Afar Basin

PS

Following the clues from the satellite image, White's team headed into the basin to examine these patches of sediment. The dirt road switchbacked down the side of the rift, which is a crack in the earth that formed 30 million years ago. Trees and grass grew thinner as the team drove deeper down the hillside. At the bottom of the basin they found a flat plain scarred with lines. The earth shifts along these lines, lifting and tipping huge blocks of rocks. The Awash River snakes through this land. The Ayelu volcano stands like a guard over the southeast horizon, and at its feet sits Yardi Lake.

The village of Herto is situated on a peninsula that juts into this lake. Among the grass-covered huts and thorny bushes, White's team found scattered pieces of fossilized animal bones and stone tools. The scientists carefully surveyed the ground a few hundred yards from the village. They crawled around on their hands and knees, scouting for fossils and artifacts while remaining on the lookout for the crocodiles that inhabit the lake.

On November 16, 1997, White's team got lucky. They spotted a fragment of a human skull. The scientists used GPS to identify the longitude and latitude of the fossil and they marked it with a yellow flag.

Because ancient fossils are so fragile, the researchers injected a hardener into the sediment and covered it with a plastic cast. Once the sediment hardened, they dug up the entire block of dirt in which the fossil was buried. Then they transported it to the National Museum of Ethiopia, where the bones were painstakingly removed from the sediment using delicate tools, such as dental picks and porcupine quills.

[Slowly, anatomists reconstructed an almost complete skull from the Herto bones.]

The scientists believe the skull belonged to a male. His brow ridge was not much thicker than that on modern humans, and his brain cavity was actually slightly larger than ours is today. Experts concluded that the ancient people who lived at Herto were *Homo sapiens*. However, they gave these prehistoric people an extra label to distinguish them from modern humans—*idaltu*. The word means "elder" in the Afar language. This skull is between 160,000 and 154,000 years old and is one of the oldest *Homo sapiens* fossils ever found.

ARCHAEOLOGISTS AT WORK

The site at Herto eventually yielded the skulls of another adult and a child, as well as 640 stone tools. When the tools were unearthed, archaeologists entered the picture. They have the expertise to understand what the hand axes, stone flakes, and blades reveal about the prehistoric people who once lived at Herto.

FOSSILS

A fossil is a preserved piece of an ancient organism. Have you ever seen a dinosaur fossil? Humans can leave fossils, too. After a person dies, the protein and fat in the bones are consumed by bacteria. Over time, as water percolates through the soil and into the spongy bone, the bone becomes rock-like. To date, scientists around the world have found the skeleton remains of more than 6,000 prehistoric people.

TOOLS FOR ARCHAEOLOGISTS

Archaeologists use a variety of tools in the field to ensure they are treating the artifacts as carefully as possible. Watch the supervising archaeologist for the National Geographic program, *Diggers*, talk about the tools of his trade on this website.

National Geographic *Diggers*

Archaeology is the study of all of the stuff that humans make. This includes the trash we throw away and the artistic masterpieces we create. Archaeologists analyze artifacts to learn how humans from past eras interacted socially, what technology they used, what they believed, and why and how they migrated. The stone tools unearthed at Herto were the same basic kind of tools that prehistoric humans had been making for tens of thousands of years. However, scientists discovered one fossil that suggests an important change was occurring—the Herto people may have been engaging in symbolic behavior.

Scientists found the skull of a six-year-old child that bore signs of cut marks. These marks indicated the flesh had been removed from the bone not long after the child died, when the tissue was still fresh. Also, the skull was smooth and polished. Certain peoples in New Guinea practice a type of skull respectfulness today. Archaeologists hypothesized that the people of Herto used this child's skull in the same way. Perhaps the fossil had such a polished surface because it had been passed from person to person, for many years, in some kind of ritual.

This hypothesis can never be proven. When it comes to artifacts that represent a culture's symbolic beliefs, archaeologist John Shea, of Stony Brook University, says, "We can speculate, but can't test these speculations with evidence."

Archaeologists fix the age of the artifacts they find by using different dating techniques. Relative dating compares the ages of objects in relationship to each other. For example, a stone tool found close to the surface of the soil is probably younger than an object buried much deeper at the same site.

Archaeologists also date by the principle of association. If objects are found close together in the same setting, they were probably put there at the same time in history. Geophysical dating provides more precise dates. When a living thing dies—whether a human being or birch tree—the organism stops excreting carbon-14, and this isotope begins to transform into carbon-12. The amount of carbon-14 left in a fossil or artifact reveals how many years ago the organism died.

While scattered bones and stones provide a trail of prehistoric migration, it is a trail with many dead ends and unanswered questions. In the last 20 years, a new tool has emerged that helps scientists discover the missing data—deoxyribonucleic acid, or DNA.

POTASSIUM–ARGON DATING

Volcanic rock is valuable to geologists because it provides a clock by which to age fossils. Volcanic sediment contains the radioactive isotope potassium-40. As this isotope decays, it turns into argon gas. Scientists can measure the rate at which this change occurs. Therefore, the more argon gas that is present in a piece of volcanic rock, the older that rock is.

HOW OLD DO YOU THINK THEY ARE?

ARCHAEOLOGISTS HAVE MANY DATING TECHNIQUES TO ANSWER THAT QUESTION.

DATING TECHNIQUES? I'M AN EXPERT AT DATING!

SERIOUSLY?

OH YEAH, I ALMOST WENT ON A DATE ONCE!

GENETICISTS AT WORK

If you swipe the inside of your cheek with a cotton swab, you won't see anything on the swab. However, this little piece of cotton holds the history of your ancestors' migration. Have you ever read a novel or watched a movie in which detectives crack a case because the criminal left behind traces of their DNA at the scene of the crime? Geneticists study DNA to figure out how closely humans are related to each other. This evidence can help us trace prehistoric migration patterns. To understand how genetics works, let's peek inside your body.

You are made up of trillions of cells. Each cell has a nucleus, which is an egg-shaped structure that holds 46 spaghetti-shaped chromosomes. These chromosomes come in pairs. You get 23 chromosomes from your mom and 23 from your dad. One set of chromosomes determines your sex. If you're a girl, you have two X chromosomes, and if you're a boy, you have an X and a Y chromosome.

Each chromosome contains a single strand of DNA. DNA is a super-thin molecule that acts like a computer program for your body. If a molecule of DNA was stretched out, it would be more than 6 feet long. In our bodies, though, DNA molecules are packed into a space smaller than a dust speck. The core of a DNA molecule has four nucleotides, or building blocks—adenine, thymine, cytosine, and guanine (ATCG). These nucleotides are strung together in a genetic sentence that might look something like this: ATACTGGTGCTGAAT.

Your body has about 100 trillion cells. This means you are carrying around 1 billion miles of DNA inside of you. Luckily, DNA's double-helix shape does not take up much room!

Does this look like gibberish to you? That's because you can't read DNA!

Segments of DNA are called genes. The set of genes a person carries is called their genome. You inherited your genes from your parents, and they got their genome from their parents, which they received from your grandparents, and on down the line until we reach back to the very first humans at the dawn of time. The combinations formed by nucleotides are actually messages that your ancestors left in your cells.

[
Your DNA is 99.9 percent identical
to every other person on earth.
]

The remaining 0.1 percent is what makes us different from each other, such as eye color or height. Once in a great while, a gene will spontaneously change. This is called a mutation. Most mutations are harmless, but they provide what's called genetic markers. If a genetic marker is found in your DNA and in the DNA of a person living on the other side of the planet, you and this stranger must share a common ancestor. Geneticists compare markers between different populations around the world to determine how groups of people are related.

When the DNA from your parents was combined to create you, your genes were reshuffled. This blending makes it difficult for scientists to spot genetic markers. So when geneticists try to trace ancestry, they look at two regions in the cells where gene mutations are passed down unchanged, generation after generation.

TRAVEL TIPS

Geneticist Spencer Wells says, "Every drop of human blood contains a history book written in the language of our genes."

Although most DNA is packaged in chromosomes within the nucleus, mitochondria also have a small amount of their own DNA. This genetic material is known as mitochondrial DNA or mtDNA.

The mitochondrial DNA (mtDNA) is passed down in an exact replica from mother to offspring. Similarly, the Y chromosome is handed down virtually unchanged from father to son. Genetic markers in these areas of the cells can be traced back thousands of generations to the very first ancestor who had the mutation.

In the 1980s, researchers at the University of California Berkley compared mtDNA from samples of women from all over the world. They found that women in Africa had twice as many genetic mutations as women in other continents when compared to one another. Scientists know that mutations occur at a steady rate. Therefore, they concluded that women have lived twice as long in Africa as anywhere else on the planet. This fits with archaeological and anthropological evidence, which shows that human beings first evolved in Africa.

Now that we have a basic understanding of genetics, archaeology, and paleoanthropology, it is time to track the path of human migration around the world. Let us begin at the beginning—Africa.

KEY QUESTIONS

- What are some of the ways scientists determine the age of an ancient artifact?

- Why do we study our ancestors? What can we learn from the ancient past that might be useful in our present-day lives?

- What are some of the challenges researchers face when studying the bones of people who lived more than 100,000 years ago?

TRAIT INVENTORY

Traits are observable characteristics that we inherit from our parents. Different traits are common among different populations. Complete the following trait inventory with friends to see how similar and different you are.

- **Divide your group into pairs.** Have each person take an inventory of the observable traits in his or her partner. These include sex, attached earlobes, right-handedness, curly hair, ability to roll one's tongue, ability to see red and green colors, crossing left thumb over right when clasping hands, dimples, cleft chin, hitchhiker's thumb, hair on the middle of fingers. Plot the results on the wall graph.

- **Discuss the results.** How are you most similar? Most different? Estimate how many traits you would need to explore before someone in the group was unique. Which of your traits could be changed by interaction with the environment? How? What are the benefits of some genetic variation? What are some potential problems it can cause?

To investigate more, select a specific trait to research. How is this trait passed on? What variations of this trait can be seen in human populations around the world? What are the survival advantages or disadvantages of this trait? How does this trait interact with the environment? To explore the relationship between race and genetic variation, go to this website.

 understanding race

Ideas for Supplies

- group of friends or classmates
- inventory list of physical traits
- colored dot stickers
- large, wall-sized bar graph with number of students on the y-axis and the inventory traits on the x-axis

VOCAB LAB

Write down what you think each word means:

paleoanthropologist, **symbolic behavior**, **artifact, sediment**, **nucleotides, geneticist**, and **isotope**.

Compare your definitions with those of your friends or classmates. Did you all come up with the same meanings? Turn to the text and glossary if you need help.

Chapter Two
Out of Africa

What factors contributed to humans leaving the continent of Africa?

Early humans might have left Africa for many reasons, including the desire for more space, the need for food, and simple curiosity about the world beyond their borders.

The Indian Ocean surges against the rocky coastline of the southern tip of Africa. Blombos Cave sits perched on a limestone cliff that overlooks the surf. Inside the cave, a reddish-brown stone about 3 inches long peeks out of the sand. Its surface is polished and smooth. On the stone is a series of crossed lines. This design was not carved by the sea or the sand or the wind. It was made by human hands about 70,000 years ago.

Who was the prehistoric artist and why did he or she create this object? Was it a caveman's doodle or part of a religious ritual? We might never know. We do know that this piece of carved red ocher is one of the oldest known works of art.

The artist in Blombos Cave lived in the midst of a revolution in the prehistoric world. *Homo sapiens* were becoming strong enough, curious enough, and culturally supported enough to venture out of Africa in the next step on modern human's path to world domination.

To understand how and why some humans ventured off the African continent, we must first unravel the complex story of how humans evolved.

WHAT DOES IT MEAN TO BE HUMAN?

Are you more closely related to a sparrow or a spider? A chimpanzee or a Chihuahua? The woman who lives next door or the man who lives a continent away? Scientists classify all living things according to how similar they are to each other. For example, you belong to the primate order—a category you share with chimpanzees, orangutans, gorillas, and others. All of these animals, including you, have forward-facing eyes, opposable thumbs, and big brains. You share a common ancestor with chimpanzees that lived in Africa more than 6 million years ago.

[While the DNA of a human and a chimpanzee only varies by 1.2 percent, we are very different creatures.]

During millions of years, humans and other primates took different evolutionary paths. Evolution is the process by which a species changes form throughout generations. A sudden change in a gene or chromosome, called a mutation, is the flame that ignites the evolutionary spark. Mutations are passed down from parent to child.

If a mutation helps the animal survive and reproduce, this change spreads throughout the population. For example, approximately 4 million years ago, one of our apelike ancestors underwent changes made possible by a complex set of mutations that enabled him to regularly walk upright. This trait, called bipedalism, is something only humans do among the great apes.

HOMO ERECTUS

When scientists began to discover fossils of prehistoric animals that walked upright, they grouped them into a category called a family. All bipedal primates belong to the hominin family. One of the earliest bipedal hominins was *Homo erectus*. *Homo* means "man" in Latin, which is the language of science. *Homo erectus* became part of a subdivision of the hominin family called the genus.

The fossil record suggests that bipedalism was the first distinctly human trait. Large brains came in a close second. When hominins first evolved in Africa about 6 million years ago, their brains were the same size as a chimpanzee's, which is much smaller than our brains are today. Brain size grew slowly during the next 4 million years. Then, from 800,000 to 200,000 years ago, hominin brains experienced a growth spurt. Bigger brains gave prehistoric humans major advantages over small-brained creatures. They could store decades of information, make split-second decisions, and solve problems.

Problem-solving skills are evident in another distinctly human trait—tool making. By 2.6 million years ago, hominins in East Africa used flaked stone tools to butcher large mammals, although they probably scavenged dead animals rather than hunting live ones. Slowly and steadily, human mental abilities became more advanced.

By 790,000 years ago, human ancestors had harnessed the power of fire. By 500,000 years ago, they had created long spears to hunt large mammals. Then, around 100,000 years ago, technology exploded. Tools made from bone, ivory, and antlers appear alongside stone spear tips and arrowheads. Humans sewed furs into clothing. They invented hooks and learned to fish. And, like the artist in Blombos Cave, they created art.

All prehistoric hominins with modern anatomical features belong to the genus *Homo*.

A prehistoric tool called a Clovis point

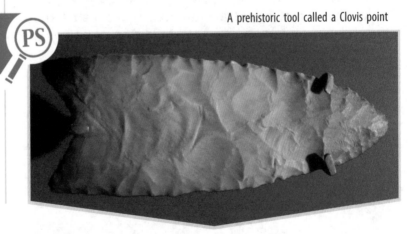

These inventors belong to the species *sapiens*. A species is the narrowest category in the scientific classification system. Two organisms from the same species must be able to reproduce offspring that resemble its parents. The term *Homo sapiens* translates to "wise person."

BRANCHES ON THE HUMAN FAMILY TREE

The trunk of the family tree is rooted in Africa and it branches off in many directions. Some of the 23 hominin species on this tree retained many ape-like qualities and became evolutionary dead-ends, but members of the genus *Homo* continued to evolve and migrated out of Africa. These prehistoric ancestors are *Homo erectus*, *Homo heidelbergensis*, and *Homo neanderthalensis*.

Homo erectus was the first hominin to physically resemble modern humans. He had a slender torso, long legs, and proportional arms. Around 1.9 million years ago, *Homo erectus* began to leave Africa, and during the course of hundreds of thousands of years, he migrated into Asia. His fossil record ends about 143,000 years ago. This species lived on the earth nine times longer than modern humans have been in existence.

Our ancient grandmother many times over might have been *Homo heidelbergensis*. She evolved in Africa around 600,000 years ago. With a larger brain capacity than ours, this early human was the first to routinely hunt large animals and was the first to build wood and rock shelters. *H. heidelbergensis* migrated to Asia and then Europe. Around 300,000 years ago, the *H. heidelbergensis* in Europe mutated and our closest relative was born—*Homo neanderthalensis*.

NEANDERTHAL MAN

Neanderthals have been the stereotype of a caveman since their bones were first discovered in Germany in 1856. This prehistoric human was short and stocky, with a barrel chest, an ape-like forehead, and a gigantic nose. Neanderthals lived in Europe and Asia between 400,000 and 28,000 years ago, surviving during a frigid time when about 30 percent of the earth was covered in ice.

Neanderthals developed advanced technology. They used spears to hunt large mammals and dressed in animal hides. Painted shells were discovered at a Neanderthal site in Spain, suggesting that Neanderthals were developing a more complex culture. However, they did not get a chance to see where this culture would lead. About 28,000 years ago, on an isolated rock island between Spain and North Africa, the last Neanderthal colony died out. Only one hominin species was left standing.

HOW DID MODERN HUMANS LEAVE AFRICA?

Homo sapiens evolved in Africa about 200,000 years ago. Today, all 7 billion people on Earth belong to this species. Prehistoric *Homo sapiens* had slender torsos and long limbs. Their brains were about 1,500 cubic centimeters, slightly larger than ours are today, and they had a high forehead and smooth brow. If you dressed one of these Stone Age ancestors in modern clothing and put him on a city bus, he would fit right in.

There are three theories to explain how *Homo sapiens* came to dominate the world—the replacement model, the multi-regional model, and the assimilation model. The replacement model argues that modern humans evolved in Africa about 200,000 years ago, probably from *Homo heidelbergensis*. Around 60,000 years ago, some *Homo sapiens* migrated into Asia and then moved on to Europe, eventually replacing Neanderthal man. How *Homo sapiens* replaced Neanderthal is a matter of debate. Did the species wage war against each other and *Homo sapiens* won? Was there too much competition over scarce food? Did *Homo sapiens* have immunities to diseases that killed Neanderthals? We'll examine this controversy in Chapter Five.

Researchers who believe in the multi-regional model contend that *Homo sapiens* evolved simultaneously throughout the world. This theory argues that when *Homo erectus* left Africa, he continued to evolve as he migrated through Asia and into Europe, while at the same time, *Homo sapiens* were evolving in Africa. Evolutionary mutations were exchanged through interbreeding as prehistoric peoples migrated back and forth between Africa, Europe, and Asia.

Multi-regionalists maintain that skeletons provide support for their theory. They point to the heavy brow ridge of many Europeans that resembles Neanderthal man's forehead, and the shovel-shaped incisors of people in East Asia that are similar to the teeth of *Homo erectus*. Some fossils found in China suggest that *Homo sapiens* were present in Asia as far back as 100,000 years ago, far earlier than previously believed. Multi-regionalists say that these fossils prove that humans were evolving in different places at the same time.

The assimilation model argues that humans did evolve their modern physical traits in Africa, but they did not take over the world by simply replacing other prehistoric humans.

TRAVEL TIPS

Multi-regionalists believe that the common ancestor of modern humans was a *Homo erectus* who lived in Africa about 1.8 million years ago.

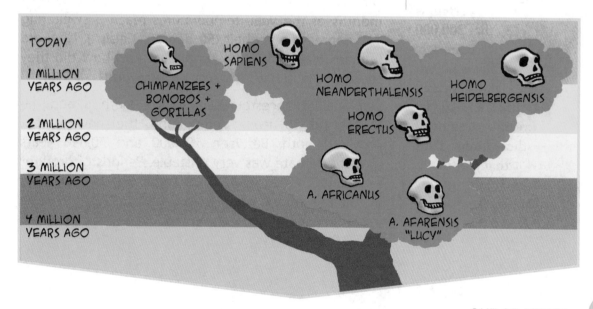

What is known for certain is that 200,000 years ago, *Homo sapiens* appeared in Africa, and 60,000 years ago, some of these humans left that continent. Slowly and steadily they migrated across the entire planet.

Instead, the traits of *Homo neanderthalensis* and *Homo heidelbergensis* were gradually assimilated into the *Homo sapiens* population through interbreeding. Genetic evidence has bolstered the assimilation model. In 2006, the DNA of a Neanderthal fossil was sequenced and compared to the DNA of modern humans. All non-African humans today carry small amounts of Neanderthal DNA.

Which of the theories about how *Homo sapiens* came to be the master of planet is correct? Each model has supporting evidence. However, every new fossil that is discovered and each time genetic technology is advanced, the debate changes. This is both the beauty and the frustration of science. Each answer leads to more questions.

LEAVING HOME

For prehistoric humans, Africa was geographically difficult to leave. Vast, impassable oceans lay to the west, south, and east. The Saharan Desert engulfed the northern part of the continent. Winds in this desert can reach hurricane strength and during the hottest months of the year, temperatures reach a sweltering 122 degrees Fahrenheit (50 degrees Celsius). How did humans make it off the continent? And how did they survive to populate the rest of the world?

Our ancient ancestors needed the method and the motivation to leave Africa, and the environment provided both. Between 100,000 and 70,000 years ago, the climate was very unstable. Periods of drought alternated with heavy rains and floods. Extremes in climate might have forced humans to be more inventive.

Evidence for this is a technological explosion that shows up in artifacts dated back to 70,000 years ago. Carved stone, inscribed ostrich shells, ornamental shell beads, throwing spears and arrows, the use of fire to clear land, and trade networks all reveal that humans were developing creative problem-solving skills.

These skills were vital for survival. The chipped and flaked stone tools of their ancestors were not going to cut it in an environment that fluctuated rapidly. It was a dangerous time for the human race.

> Scientists believe that the population of *Homo sapiens* in Africa dropped down to less than 10,000 people. We were on our way to extinction.

One of the new technologies humans developed at this time was fishing. Prehistoric sites in southern Africa are full of seashell remains. This change in behavior might have sparked a change in biology as well.

Some archaeologists speculate that once humans learned how to fish, the fatty acids in the seafood gave them the nutritional trigger they needed to jump-start their brains. University of Cape Town archaeologist John Parkington claims that this nutritional boost "is the evolutionary driving force. It is sucking people into being more cognitively aware, faster-wired, faster-brained, smarter."

But why did humans choose to leave Africa at this time? They might have wanted more elbow room. The climate finally started to stabilize around 60,000 years ago and, combined with adaptations that helped them flourish, the population rebounded.

THE PREHISTORIC FINGER

In 2013, a 40,000-year-old finger bone and molar were discovered in a cave in Siberia. DNA analysis showed that the bone did not come from a Neanderthal or a *Homo sapiens*. It was a completely new species. Scientists named the fossil Denisovan after the cave in which it was found. It turns out that modern humans bred with Denisovans as well as Neanderthals. The DNA of people from New Guinea is 6 percent Denisovan.

TRAVEL TIPS

Some researchers suspect that a genetic mutation led to increased brainpower.

The debate about what route the first migrants took out of Africa reveals the challenges of unraveling the story of prehistoric migration. There are gaps in evidence. Data is open to interpretation. A scientist's background affects the value they place on discoveries.

At this time, people lived by hunting and gathering. As population increased, competition for resources might have pushed some daring explorers to take their chances by venturing into new land. Humans might also have left Africa for the same reason people travel today. Bence Viola, of the Max Planck Institute for Evolutionary Anthropology, says, "Curiosity is a pretty human desire."

Two possible routes lay open to these prehistoric pioneers. The northern route led up the Nile valley through present-day Egypt and present-day Djibouti, across the Sinai Peninsula, and into the Middle East. The southern route went from the Horn of Africa, across the Bab el-Mandeb Strait to the Arabian Peninsula. Which route humans took is the subject of intense debate among scientists.

A trail of stone tools is evidence for the southern route. Today, the distance across the Bab el-Mandeb Strait is about 20 miles. However, during the last Ice Age, the Red Sea was lower. There was only 2.5 miles of water. Between 150,000 and 130,000 years ago, Nubian toolmakers in the Nile River Valley were crude toolmakers. They chipped the edges of a stone core to form a triangular spear point. But by 50,000 years ago, humans had developed the Emiran tool kit, a major leap forward. Points, blades, and scrappers found in a cave in Israel reveal that toolmakers had discovered how to cut many elongated blades from one stone core.

In 2015, archaeologists Jeffrey Rose, of the Ronin Institute, and Anthony Marks, of the Southern Methodist University, reported that they had discovered tools on the Arabia Peninsula that are offshoots of the Nubian tool kit. These artifacts are evidence that after people left Africa, they moved to Arabia and adapted their technology to suit the changing environment.

As the climate grew drier, large mammals disappeared and humans had to hunt lizards and rodents. To catch these speedy, small animals, humans made smaller, longer spear tips.

By 75,000 years ago, the lakes and rivers of Arabia had dried up, so people moved north into what is today Israel, where they perfected the Emiran technique. Rose and Anthony contend that the changing tool kit supports the theory that humans took the southern route out of Africa, then lingered for about 50,000 years in Arabia before heading north through Israel and on to the rest of the Middle East.

This migration out of Africa was not a marathon hike for a few brave explorers. Researchers estimate that this exodus involved anywhere from 1,000 to 50,000 people, and it probably occurred in waves. The movements north and east were incremental. If you had lived back then, you would not have even realized you were migrating once you reached Asia. Spencer Wells said, "It was less of a journey and probably more like walking a little farther down the beach to get away from the crowd." But during the course of a millennium, every step adds up.

KEY QUESTIONS

- How do physical characteristics contribute to migration? For example, would humans be more or less likely to travel if they didn't walk upright?

- Climate change is often in the news in the current world. What affect might climate change have on human migration in the future?

DNA VS. STONE

Geneticists put more stock in DNA than in pieces of stone. Spencer Wells, the founder of the National Geographic Society's Genographic Project, says that while the stone tools in Arabia are interesting, "It does not rewrite the book on what we know about human migratory history." He believes that our genes tell a clearer story of the route our ancestors took out of Africa.

In 2015, Luca Pagani, of the University of Cambridge, released the results of a study that compared the genomes of modern Egyptians, Ethiopians, and Eurasians. "What we found," Pagani explained, "is that all Eurasians are more similar to . . . Egyptians than to . . . Ethiopians, and this shows that the last stop out of Africa was . . . Egypt rather than Ethiopia." Pagani is convinced that the ancestors of modern humans left Africa on foot via the northern route.

Ideas for Supplies ▼

- several long sheets of dark-colored butcher paper
- dishpan of water
- cookie tray filled with flour or chalk powder
- strong hairspray

FOOTPRINTS IN THE SAND

A key trait that first separated hominins from other primates was bipedalism. In 1976, anthropologist Mary Leakey discovered a pair of fossilized footprints at a site called Laetoli in Tanzania, Africa. At least 3.5 million years ago, two individuals walked across wet volcanic ash. This ash hardened like cement. What can a footprint reveal about a species? Make your own footprints and discover what secrets they share about you.

- **With an adult's permission, locate images on the Internet of the hominin footprints that Mary Leakey discovered in Laetoli.** Make a list of scientific questions that the footprint fossils might be able to answer.

- **Make your own fossilized footprints. Lay out your colored butcher paper.** Remove your shoes and socks. Step in the tub of water. Step in the tray of flour or chalk powder. Walk across the butcher paper. Spray hairspray on the paper to seal your prints in place.

- **Make more sets of prints by altering your pace.** Do your prints change when you run across the paper? What about when you walk very slowly? Try walking the way a chimpanzee would if it stood upright—sort of swaying from side to side on the outsides of the feet. How does this gait change your footprint?

- **Analyze your footprints.** What physical properties of the prints helps you determine the weight, height, and sex of the person who made the prints? Is there a relationship between the length of a person's footprint and his height? How could you determine that?

To investigate more, have a group of friends create footprint patterns. Each person should identify his print paper with a symbol to keep the identity of the print maker secret. Everyone should analyze all the prints, recording conclusions about the physical traits of the person who made them. Share your conclusions with each other. How accurately did you identify the correct traits from footprints? What would you need to revise in order to reach more accurate conclusions?

VOCAB LAB

Write down what you think each word means:

assimilation, DNA, mutation, evolution, bipedalism, hominin, genus, and **species.**

Compare your definitions with those of your friends or classmates. Did you all come up with the same meanings? Turn to the text and glossary if you need help.

Fossilized footprint

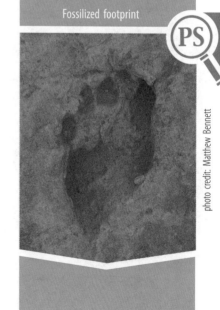

photo credit: Matthew Bennett

GLOBETROTTERS

In order to get a clear view of the migration routes of prehistoric people, plot fossil discoveries of hominin species on a world map.

Ideas for Supplies ▼

- several friends or classmates
- 8½-by-11-inch map with latitude and longitude lines marked
- oversized world map
- colored push-pins to designate the different subspecies: *Homo erectus, Homo heidelbergensis, Homo neanderthalensis, Homo sapiens*

To investigate more, continue mapping the migration patterns of humans as you read this book. Examine migration continent by continent. Is there a way to plot migration within countries to distinguish it from migration between countries?

- **Divide into pairs.** Each pair researches important prehistoric fossil discoveries for a different species in the *Homo* genus. Find longitude and latitude coordinates of each fossil discovery for your species. Plot these discoveries on your small map.

- **Use the colored push pins to plot the hominin fossils on the wall map.** How can you label the ages of the fossils on the big map? Why would it be important to know how old each fossil is?

- **Discuss the group's findings based on the plot points on the map.**

  - How would you describe the general migration pattern of prehistoric humans?

  - Which species settled most widely in Asia and Europe?

  - What inferences can you make about how humans reached the places where their fossils were discovered?

  - Are there places when different species of humans lived near each other at the same time?

  - Why do you think species overlapped in these particular places?

  - What impact might this overlap in settlement have had on each species, both culturally and physically?

  - What biological adaptions would you expect to see develop in different parts of the world?

Chapter Three
Asia to Australia

How did ancient people travel from Asia to Australia?

There is no hard evidence to determine conclusively how people got from Asia to Australia. Scientists work with competing theories about how and when ancient people made the journey.

On the island of Sumatra, which is in Indonesia between mainland Asia and Australia, strange things began to happen 74,000 years ago. The earth seemed angry. It inhaled and exhaled. Steam rose from the ground. Tremors shook Mount Toba. If anyone was watching these events, they should have run for their lives. Not that running would have saved them. Shortly after these signals occurred, the mountain exploded.

The eruption of Mount Toba was the biggest volcanic blast the world had seen for at least 2.5 million years. The mountain spewed 700 cubic miles of magma into the air, the equivalent of 19 million Empire State Buildings. A plume of ash stretched from the South China Sea to the Arabian Sea. A layer of ash blanketed the ground for 4,350 miles. The sun could not shine through this cloud of dust and gas. Within days, the trees shed their leaves and an unnatural and seemingly never-ending winter began.

The eruption of Mount Toba is a signpost on the path of human migration in Asia. There are few prehistoric artifacts on this continent for researchers to follow, and the fossil record is scant and confusing. This lack of data has led to controversy about the route humans took through Asia and when they traveled it.

[
Some scientists believe that *Homo sapiens* arrived in Asia after Mount Toba erupted, while others believe early humans passed through this region long before the volcano exploded.
]

ARRIVAL IN ASIA

Everyone likes to spend time on the beach, and early humans were no exception. One theory about migration through Asia is that *Homo sapiens* were beachcombers. This model, called the coastal express, argues that humans left Africa no earlier than 70,000 years ago, and they took about 10,000 years to migrate along the Arabian coast and the southern edges of India into Southeast Asia.

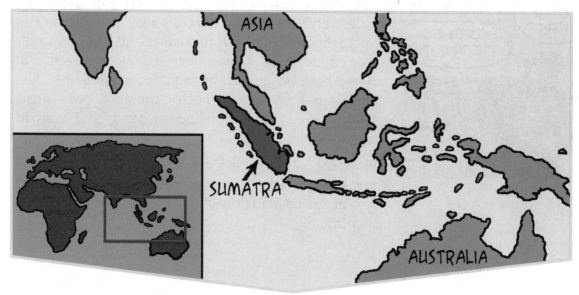

Genetic evidence backs up this theory. Professors Paul Mellars, of the University of Cambridge, and Martin Richards, of the University of Huddersfield, analyzed 1,000 genomes from people who are living in India today. Their analysis of genetic markers showed that the ancestors of these modern people did not reach Asia until less than 60,000 years ago.

It is a challenge to find archaeological evidence to back up the coastal express model because settlements on beaches are easily washed away. However, a prehistoric oyster bar has been found in Eritrea on the Horn of Africa. Buried among thousands of split oyster shells were human-made obsidian blades and the butchered remains of large mammals.

Proponents of the coastal express theory believe that if early humans crossed the Red Sea and moved only a couple miles down the beach during each generation, they could have reached Indonesia in about 10,000 years. From there, Australia is only a few island hops away.

Artifacts found from before and after the Mount Toba explosion support the idea that *Homo sapiens* arrived after the mountain exploded 74,000 years ago. The oldest artifacts in the Jurreru Valley in India and in Sri Lanka are simple stone points and scrapers, tools that could have been made by *Homo erectus* or *Homo heidelbergensis*. But tools found after the Toba explosion are suddenly much more advanced—small, finely worked blades, bone points, beads, and adorned ostrich shells.

Professor Mellars believes that this technological revolution is a sign that modern humans arrived in Asia at this point in time. And they brought their smarts with them.

However, the coastal express model has critics. Michael Petraglia, of the University of Oxford, calls Mellars's theory "baseless archaeologically." Petraglia excavated in the Jurreru Valley and found simple stone tools buried in the Toba ash that were dated between 77,000 and 74,000 years old. He argued that these were similar to the tools made by *Homo sapiens* in southern Africa. That means that *Homo sapiens* arrived in India before Toba exploded.

Petraglia is not convinced by the DNA evidence indicating that *Homo sapiens* could not have arrived in Asia before 60,000 years ago. He said, "My issue with these guys is, what are they sampling? They're sampling modern humans that live today—a small subset of what out-of-Africa was." He believes that the genetic signal of the earliest immigrants has been lost over time.

[
Both the pre-Toba and post-Toba models of migration through Asia are built on scanty evidence.
]

What scientists really need is a skeleton buried under the Toba ash, a skull that can reveal the story of how and when it got there. Such a fossil has not yet been found. However, there have been discoveries in other parts of Asia that prove that not all prehistoric migrants took the beach route through Asia. Some people chose to travel inland. Evidence of this migratory route has been found in the jungles of Southeast Asia.

Science is all about debate and collaboration between experts, but the tension can get thick between scientists whose entire careers are built upon specific theories. Archaeologist Anthony Marks says that, "People say mute stones speak. They don't. We're the ones who impose our views on them."

CAVE OF THE MONKEYS

The road from Vientiane, Laos, to Pa Hang Mountain is so rough that it takes two days to drive the 150 miles. Perched on top of Pa Hang Mountain is Tam Pa Ling cave, also known as the Cave of the Monkeys.

The cave is not easy to reach. First, you must climb the side of a cliff. Then you have to traverse 200 feet down a slope of wet clay. Watch out for the wild pigs that dart across the path! Brush aside the branches of the papaya and banana trees that surround the cave. Once inside, be on the lookout for the monkeys foraging for food.

[
The idea of finding a prehistoric ancestor in a site as remote as this seems futile, but in 2009, paleoanthropologist Laura Lynn Shackelford, of the University of Illinois, got lucky.
]

Inside the cave, Shackelford found a partial *Homo sapiens* skull, including jaw fragments and teeth. These fossils are between 46,000 and 63,000 years old, making them the earliest evidence of modern humans living outside of the Middle East. Shackelford named the fossil "Tam Pa Ling Lady."

She believes this discovery supports the coastline express model of Asian migration. Humans did follow the southern coastline as they walked from India through Southeast Asia and on to Australia. However, the Tam Pa Ling Lady suggests that these migrants took other routes, too. Early humans traveled deep into the mountains of this region, probably following the extensive river system. There are thousands of limestone caves in the jungles of Southeast Asia. Tam Pa Ling Lady's relatives might have been hiding in some of these caves.

THE HOBBIT

In 2004, scientists found human bones on the Indonesian island of Flores unlike any discovered before. These people were 3 feet tall with brains one-quarter the size of modern humans. They could make fire and hunted the giant rats and pygmy elephants that lived on the island. Researchers named the species *Homo florensis*. Because of its small size, the species was dubbed "the Hobbit" by the media. The bones are between 95,000 and 17,000 years old. The small size of this species might have come from a phenomenon called island dwarfism. In a confined environment, such as an island, smaller mammals have a survival advantage because they require less food.

THE LAND DOWN UNDER

Mungo National Park, located in a remote area of Australia, looks like Mars. Dry lakebeds are a mosaic of red and gray clay. Wind and rain have sculpted millions of years of sediment to create cathedral-like ridges and spires. Oceans of sand ripple in the dune fields with waves of loamy brown, deep white, and burnt orange.

In this place of stark and haunting beauty hides a world treasure. Five hundred footprints preserved in the clay walk straight out of the last Ice Age. These tracks represent at least 25 sets of individual tracks from both young and old people.

The 20,000-year-old tracks provide an intimate picture of a Stone Age community. One set of footprints belonged to a child. At one point, the youngster ran away from the rest of the group, paused, and then returned slowly, maybe reluctantly. Another set of prints is from a one-legged man who could hop quickly. Other artifacts and fossils in Australia reveal that humans migrated to this remote continent at least 40,000 years ago. But Australia is separated from Asia by water. So how did the first humans reach this isolated continent?

Prehistoric migrants could have walked part of the way. During the last global Ice Age, glaciers absorbed so much of the earth's water that sea levels fell as much as 400 feet. The most dramatic impact of this was seen in eastern Asia and Australia. Until 8,000 years ago, Australia, New Guinea, and Tasmania made up one huge island called Sahul. The Java and South China Seas were so low that the Malay Peninsula was linked to the islands of Sumatra, Java, and Borneo by a large forested land called Sundaland. These low seas meant that early humans could have walked most of the way to Australia.

EXPERIMENTAL ARCHAEOLOGY

Robert Bednarik is an experimental archaeologist. He constructs rafts using only the tools and techniques that Stone Age people had available. For the documentary *The Incredible Human Journey*, Bednarik took anthropologist Alice Roberts on a test drive across a 6.8-mile stretch of water in Indonesia on a raft he made from green bamboo and rattan. High waves and strong winds made the journey frightening at times, but their raft made the voyage without falling apart. You can watch *The Incredible Human Journey* here.

Bednarik *Incredible Human Journey*

However, even during the coldest part of the Ice Age, at least 50 miles of ocean separated Australia from any nearby islands. Early humans must have traveled the final leg of the journey to Australia by boat. This is a logical conclusion, but there is no archaeological evidence to support the theory that humans sailed to Australia.

> No one has ever excavated an Ice Age boat and there aren't any images on cave walls of rafts or sails.

Scientists try to test the hypothesis that the first migrants reached Australia by boat in other ways. They begin by asking whether prehistoric migrants had the technology to make boats. Early humans had stone knives and axes. They had vines to make rope. And they had bamboo—a flexible, strong wood that could be used to construct a raft. They were capable of making boats, but the boats would have rotted away millennia ago.

For many years, scientists believed that humans arrived in Australia only about 20,000 years ago, long after people had already migrated to northern Asia and Europe. The Aborigines of Australia disagreed. Their ancient roots on the continent are part of their creation stories. Today, archaeological and genetic evidence proves that the Aborigines were correct. The lineage of these native people can be traced back to the humans who left Africa between 60,000 and 70,000 years ago.

Mungo Lake, in a remote corner of Australia, used to be a paradise, a rich hunting ground for prehistoric people. About 20,000 years ago, the lake dried up.

In 1974, geologist Jim Bowler was driving his motorcycle over the dry lakebed when he saw white bones sticking out of the sand. Bowler pulled a 42,000-year-old cranium from the sand. It had been stained with red ocher. Since there are no ocher deposits within 60 miles of this site, Bowler knew this pigment had to have been brought in. The man's corpse had been laid out as though in a coffin. Bowler nicknamed the bones "Mungo Man."

Bowler had also discovered the remains of a woman slightly younger than Mungo Man nearby. Her bones had been broken and burned, which is evidence of cremation. This reveals that prehistoric people had a sophisticated culture in this isolated corner of this isolated continent.

DNA provides clues for when the Mungos arrived in Australia. In 1923, British anthropologists studied a group of full-blooded Aborigines and took hair samples from one of the men. This hair was then stored and forgotten. Decades later, Danish researcher Eske Willerslev sequenced the genome from the man.

[
The results show that the genetic line of these Australians is different from the line that leads to East Asians and Europeans.
]

This means that when these migrants reached the tip of Asia, they did not turn around because they faced a vast ocean. Instead, they adapted to life on the coast. Around 55,000 years ago, a group of migrants made the voyage to Australia. These travelers remained isolated on this continent, while other waves of migrants went on to populate Asia and then move into Europe.

Mungo Man

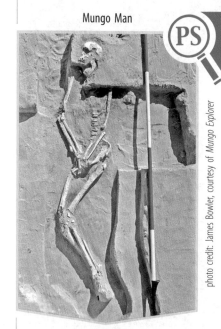

photo credit: James Bowler, courtesy of *Mungo Explorer*

KEY QUESTIONS

- What evidence is there to support the coastal express theory?

- What evidence supports the theory that humans lived in Australia before Mount Toba blew?

- What significance does the fact that scientists might never be able to prove or disprove different theories have for the study of archaeology?

Ideas for Supplies ▼

- items that will both float and remain stable
- something to tie the raft together
- something to make the raft platform
- objects to represent people

Write down what you think each word means:

coastal express, technological revolution, controversy, collaboration, confined environment, creation story, and **cremation.**

Compare your definitions with those of your friends or classmates. Did you all come up with the same meanings? Turn to the text and glossary if you need help.

WHAT FLOATS YOUR BOAT?

Researchers speculate that prehistoric migrants built bamboo rafts to travel from mainland Asia to Australia. Test your engineering skills by designing a model raft from materials you have readily available. Your raft must both float and be strong enough to carry objects that simulate the weight of passengers.

- **Brainstorm ideas for your raft design.** What materials can you use that will help your raft float and stay level? Is the comfort of the passengers an important thing to consider? How about safety?

- **Develop a hypothesis about which materials and raft design will best float and carry the most weight.** Create a record-keeping sheet to record your designs and results.

- **Build your raft and test it in a full bathtub.** Revise your design as needed based on your results.

- **Try creating a "storm" in your bathtub ocean by making waves.** How do different designs and materials hold up to this rough weather?

To investigate more, consider what would happen if you built a boat instead of a raft. How would the shape of the boat impact its buoyancy? What would happen if you used a more dense material to make the raft platform, such as clay or wood? Does this improve the raft's performance? Can you make a raft with only a limited number of supplies? If these supplies become damaged, repair them. How does this restriction affect your results?

An object floats because of density and buoyancy. Density is a measurement of how heavy an object is for the amount of space it takes up. Buoyancy is the upward force that keeps things floating. An object will float in water if its buoyancy is greater than its weight. You can increase the buoyancy of something by increasing the surface area that the water has to push against. For example, if you are in a pool of water and you curl up into a tight ball, you'll sink. But if you stretch out your arms and legs and lay flat, you'll float.

INCREASE SURFACE AREA,
INCREASE BUOYANCY

Ideas for Supplies ▼

- natural paintbrushes, such as sticks with different shaped edges, leaves from plants that you can cut and shred, hair, tubes to blow paint through

- natural pigments, such as colored rocks, dried clay, crushed bricks, crushed berries, charcoal

- rock surface on which to paint or a brown paper bag

MODERN ART

Stone Age artists used materials found in their surroundings to create masterpieces that have lasted for tens of thousands of years. Create your own natural art supplies and images to communicate a message to the future.

- **Look on the Internet for examples of prehistoric rock art.** This *Smithsonian* magazine website is a good place to start.

Smithsonian prehistoric art world

- **Think of an event from your life that you want to portray.** Do you want to show something exciting, something happy, or something sad? What event represents the time you're living in?

- **Develop symbols to communicate that event.** Ancient artists often used stick figures and signs to show who was doing what in the scenes they painted.

- **Prepare your paint by grinding pigments against a large, flat rock.** Mix water or egg yolk into the pigment until it reaches the right consistency.

- **Paint your masterpiece.** Don't forget to add a sign for your signature!

> To investigate more, try to represent abstract ideas, such as your religious, moral, or political views. Is this more difficult to do than painting scenes? What are some of the symbols you use for these abstract ideas? Do you think people will recognize them in another century?

Chapter Four
Out of the Old World and Into the New

When and how did early humans arrive in the Americas?

Just as with many early human migration stories, there are more questions than answers about human migration into the Americas.

In 1939, archaeologist Robert Wetzel discovered 200 fragments of a carved mammoth tusk in the Hohlenstein-Stadel Cave in Germany. Before he could piece them together, World War II erupted. The bone fragments sat untouched in a box for three decades. Finally, in 1963, archaeologist Joachim Hahn glued the bone fragments back together.

What emerged was a fantastical creature—part human and part lion. Experts estimate that this 40,000-year-old statue took 400 hours to carve. The Lion Man and other pieces of exquisite art made tens of thousands of years ago help explain why *Homo sapiens* are the sole surviving humans.

For thousands of years after *Homo sapiens* left Africa and spread through Asia, the climate prevented them from migrating to Europe. The routes north and west were too cold and too dry.

Then, around 52,000 years ago, the weather became dramatically warmer and wetter. A corridor of fertile land opened up in the Middle East, and people traveled this green highway from South Asia through Turkey and into southern Europe. A later migration of mammoth hunters made their way west from Central Asia into Russia and Germany.

[
When these people arrived in Europe, they found it already occupied by their cousins—Neanderthal Man.
]

HOMO SAPIENS AND NEANDERTHALS

Why and how *Homo sapiens* managed to swell in numbers and take over the planet while Neanderthals dwindled and died out is one of the persistent mysteries in paleoanthropology. The traditional story is that the *Homo sapiens* that tromped into Europe beginning 50,000 years ago were just plain smarter and tougher than the Neanderthals who were already living there. In the battle for scarce resources, we won and they lost. End of story.

Satellite view of the Fertile Crescent

photo credit: NASA

BROWN SKIN AND BLUE EYES

Mutations in skin, eye, and hair color helped people survive in prehistoric times. In Africa, dark-colored skin provided protection from damaging ultraviolet rays from the sun. But, as people moved into colder climates, light-colored skin allowed the body to absorb the ultraviolet rays needed to synthesize vitamin D. Scientists long believed that this mutation went way back to the first European migrants, around 40,000 years ago. However, genetic tests on the 7,000-year-old bones of a skeleton found in Spain revealed that although he had the gene for blue eyes, his hair was dark and his skin was brown. Scientists now hypothesize that the light-skin mutation was brought to Europe with the first farmers from the Middle East around 8,000 years ago.

PS

Not so fast! The more genetic and archaeological data scientists discover, the more that old narrative falls apart. First, Neanderthals were no dummies. While they did not make the same tools as modern humans, some Neanderthal tools were ingenious.

For example, at a site in France, scientists found a slender bone tool whose function was a mystery until they showed it to a French woman who makes saddles using traditional hand techniques. She immediately recognized the tool as a scraper used to waterproof an animal hide. This modern craftswoman uses a similar tool today. For most of the time that Neanderthals lived in Europe, the continent was gripped by a brutal Ice Age. Animal fur was the necessary fashion! Neanderthals knew how to keep themselves warm.

Not only did Neanderthals make practical tools, they were also capable of symbolic thought and symbolic behavior. Shells with pigments inside of them have been found at Neanderthal sites. Archaeologists speculate that the Neanderthals might have used the shells as bowls in which to mix paint colors to adorn the body. Perhaps they blended a sort of prehistoric makeup to represent status or for use in religious rituals.

Neanderthals also made jewelry. Polished fox teeth with holes pierced in them as though to hold a chain have been discovered alongside Neanderthal fossils at sites in Europe. Tools, makeup, jewelry—these sound like behaviors we might find in communities in the twenty-first century!

TWO BECOME ONE

If Neanderthals had such a complex culture, why did they go extinct? Part of the answer can be found in a cave in Romania. In 2002, João Zilhão, of the University of Barcelona, excavated a chamber deep inside another cave. To get to the chamber, his team had to don helmets with headlights and wade into a frigid mountain stream. The 100-percent humidity created a perpetual fog, and the temperature plunged to 50 degrees Fahrenheit. The ceiling lowered so sharply that the team had to put on facemasks and swim through an 80-foot-long underwater tunnel to reach the next chamber.

When the team emerged from the tunnel, they had to climb a series of cliffs and squeeze through a 10-foot-long narrow passage. Finally, the team emerged in the inner chamber where they could begin their excavations.

The floor of the chamber was littered with bones that were thousands of years old. Most of them were cave bear. However, Zilhão's team also found the fossilized remains of three people who lived 35,000 years ago. These fossils had a mix of features. In some respects, they were clearly modern humans—they had full chins, no brow ridges, and high, round brain cases. But they also had Neanderthal features—huge faces, a bone crest behind their ears, and gigantic wisdom teeth.

According to Zilhão, these first Europeans were hybrids. While scientists today might identify *Homo sapiens* and *Homo neanderthalensis* as different species, people living 40,000 years ago would not have thought that way.

TRAVEL TIPS

Archaeology can be a dangerous job! In Belize, scientists don scuba diving equipment and dodge crocodiles and submerged trees as they dive into pools 200-feet deep to learn about the ancient Maya. A team in Wyoming battles forest fires, floods, and an angry bear to reach Native American settlements more than 1.8 miles high in the Wind River Mountain Range. Extreme archaeology has even become the subject of reality television shows.

TRAVEL TIPS

Svante Pääbo compared the challenge of sequencing the Neanderthal genome with trying to read a book that has been ripped into a million pieces. Shred an English dictionary. Add the shredded dictionaries of many other languages, and dump a bunch of chemicals on the shredded pages. Then try to piece together the English words into logical sentences. That is how complicated it was to read the DNA of Neanderthal.

This idea of modern humans mating with Neanderthals does not fit the long-accepted explanation for how *Homo sapiens* came to be the only humans alive today. But DNA is helping convince scientists to rethink that story and give Neanderthals the status they deserve. Svante Pääbo and his team at the Max Planck Institute cracked the Neanderthal gene code in 2010. When the computer systems finally spit out the results after two and a half years of analysis, everyone had the same burning question—what happened when *Homo sapiens* and *Homo neanderthalensis* met? The answer surprised Pääbo.

Like most scientists, Pääbo had believed the narrative that *Homo sapiens* had replaced the Neanderthal population by conquest or by being smarter and more adaptable. But, Pääbo says, ". . . the power of genetics is in the way that data will stare you in the face and force you to rethink your ideas if you are wrong." The data shows that when Neanderthals and *Homo sapiens* encountered each other in Europe, they did not fight each other. Instead, they formed families. Today, the DNA of all non-African humans is between 1 and 3 percent Neanderthal.

[The Neanderthal species did not die out. We are Neanderthal.]

Recent fossil evidence supports the genetic argument that the early *Homo sapiens* mated with *Homo neanderthalensis*. Around 55,000 years ago, *Homo sapiens* were expanding out of Africa, while at the same time, Neanderthals were moving south to escape a cold spell in Europe. The two groups met in the Middle East.

At Mamot Cave in Israel, scientists have unearthed a skull that has a lump at the base—the occipital bun—that is found in both European Neanderthals and *Homo sapiens* in Africa. Also in 2013, researchers at a site in northern Italy reported on what they believed was the offspring of *Homo sapiens* and Neanderthals. The skull had both *Homo sapiens* and Neanderthal features, but its mitochondrial DNA was Neanderthal. This suggests that this person had a *Homo sapiens* father and a Neanderthal mother. Tool artifacts indicate that both *Homo sapiens* and Neanderthals lived in this area of Italy around the same time period.

While Neanderthals cured furs and made sturdy spears and axes and blades, *Homo sapiens* created masterpieces such as the Lion Men. A miniature Lion Man was discovered at a campsite 30 miles away from the cave where the large statue was found. This evidence shows that *Homo sapiens* had social connections. They spoke the same language, had similar belief systems, and traded with each other.

[
There is no evidence of any
Neanderthal settlements engaging
in such social behavior.
]

An ivory figurine of a woman was discovered in the Hohle Fels Cave in Germany. This 35,000-year-old prehistoric Venus is the oldest sculpture of the human body anywhere in the world. It's possible that it symbolized the importance of fertility and reproduction for people who struggled to survive in a harsh climate. Similar Venus figurines show up in other places in Europe.

WHERE ARE NEANDERTHALS?

Look around the world. None of us looks like a Neanderthal. If we have skeletal evidence that suggests Neanderthals and *Homo sapiens* interbred, and if we have genetic data that proves non-African people today carry small traces of Neanderthal DNA in our veins, then where are Neanderthals today? Except for that hint of Neanderthal in our DNA, we are all *Homo sapiens*. Why did the Neanderthals all but vanish?

What does art have to do with survival of a species? These artifacts prove that *Homo sapiens* communicated across long distances and were developing a set of cultural beliefs that linked people together across the European continent.

Social networks are important to survival. In times of trouble, you want to be able to rely on other people to give you shelter or share food or help you make sense of your struggles. Neanderthals did not network. Their communities remained small and isolated. When times became tough, they were alone and vulnerable.

Neanderthals did not have the technology or creativity or social skills of the *Homo sapiens* migrants, and they did not have their numbers either. Once the first *Homo sapiens* followed the Danube River from the Black Sea into Germany, the migrants kept coming. This central zone between ice sheets and mountains became a densely populated region of prehistoric Europe. Neanderthals had always been a small population, maybe only a few thousand people in the entire continent. They were outnumbered and out-networked.

Neanderthals did not vanish. Instead, they were genetically and culturally absorbed. Today, we still use some Neanderthal technology and we still carry some Neanderthal genes. But 28,000 years ago, *Homo sapiens* had the world to themselves. They looked around and decided once again to pack their bags and continue their human journey.

CAVE TOUR

The Lascaux Caves in France, which are full of 20,000-year-old rock wall paintings, are closed to the public. The breath from tourists was destroying the art, so the caves were closed. However, you can take a virtual tour of this masterpiece.

 Lascaux Caves

ROUTE TO AMERICA: A MYSTERY IN HISTORY

There is a mystery that has stumped experts for decades. How and when did the first people arrive in the Americas? The theory that was widely believed for most of the twentieth century was known as Clovis First, which represented a perfect pairing of archaeology and climate science.

In 1933, archaeologists uncovered an ancient spearhead in a dried-up lake in Clovis, New Mexico. Next to the spearhead was the skeleton of the mammoth that the spear had brought down. The mammoth bones were 13,500 years old, which meant the spearhead was the oldest artifact ever found in the Americas.

This spearhead had a distinctive design. Flakes of stone had been removed from both sides of its base. These flutes allowed the hunter to insert a wooden shaft into the stone point. Both sides of the tip had been flaked until they were razor sharp. Similar stone tips have been found throughout the United States and in Mexico, Belize, and Costa Rica. Archaeologists gave the people who made this technology their own name—the Clovis culture.

In its time, the Clovis point represented a technological breakthrough in hunting. In fact, within a few hundred years after the arrival of Clovis hunters in North America, all the prehistoric mega animals, such as the giant sloth and giant armadillo, had gone extinct. For many years, scientists believed that the migrating hunters hunted these large animals to extinction. However, new research indicates that climate change and environmental stress may have killed off most of these species.

GETTING FROM THERE TO HERE

Consider the information you have read so far. Prehistoric migrants faced difficult routes in earlier parts of their journey across the globe. What routes did the first Africans take when they left that continent? How did people reach Australia? Look at an interactive map of pre-Clovis sites in North America. If the ice-free corridor from Alaska into the North American continent was not passable until 14,000 to 13,500 years ago, how else could prehistoric migrants have reached North America from Asia and Europe before this time?

NOVA pre-Clovis sites

Who were these big game hunters and where did they come from? Scientists looked for answers in the prehistoric climate. Between 24,000 and 13,000 years ago, the world was in the grip of the last Ice Age. The gigantic glaciers locked up vast amounts of water, causing the sea levels to drop so low that the continental shelf between Siberia and Alaska was exposed. Asia and North America essentially became one large continent, connected by a 1,000-mile-wide land bridge known as Beringia. People were able to walk from the west to the east, but when they reached Alaska, they had to stop. Giant ice sheets barred their entrance to the rest of North America.

The Ice Age began to thaw, the glaciers receded, and an ice-free corridor opened. It was long believed that this door to the New World cracked open around 13,500 years ago—the same time the Clovis culture appears in North America. The Clovis First theory is that 13,500 years ago, hunters from Siberia, armed with cutting-edge technology, walked across the Bering Land Bridge into North America. They followed the ice-free corridor south and traveled down into the continent, eventually migrating deep into South America. Their descendants are Native Americans.

Clovis First makes a perfect story, and for a very long time, everyone believed that this was how the peopling of America began. However, new discoveries became too compelling to ignore. Toward the end of the twentieth century, some scientists began to question the Clovis model.

HELLO, EVA

One discovery that could not be ignored was a young woman who has been dead for about 13,500 years. Her body was discovered underwater in a vast cave in the Yucatan Peninsula in Mexico. Scientists named the woman Eva of Naharon. Eva was a member of a nomadic culture that lived in the forest about 40 miles from the cave. The cause of Eva's death is unknown, but based on the position of her body, scientists know that someone carried her to the cave, which was dry at the time, and buried her.

[
She lay undisturbed and alone until her body was discovered in 2008.
]

Eva's story is sad, but it's not the tragedy of her young death that niggles at the brains of scientists. The problem Eva poses for the mystery of human migration is how she could have lived as far south and east as the Yucatan Peninsula 13,500 years ago, when the ice-free corridor into North America had only just opened.

To further complicate the puzzle, Eva is not the only evidence that people lived in the Americas before the corridor opened. Monte Verde is an archaeological site way down on the tip of Chile in South America. Under a peat bog, scientists discovered the remains of a 60-foot-long wooden structure that could have housed up to thirty people. The daily life of this community of prehistoric inhabitants is evident in two hearths with preserved meat and firewood and three human footprints hardened in clay.

Charcoal from the Monte Verde hearths has been dated at more than 14,500 years old, far older than the land bridge of Beringia.

Once scientists accepted the possibility that Clovis First was not the full explanation, they began to find data that demonstrates the earliest migrants to North America came in different waves, at different times, and by different routes.

TRAVEL TIPS

In 2011, archaeologists announced that they had found evidence of a human settlement along the Buttermilk Creek near Austin, Texas, that is at least 15,500 years old. This find helps make it clear that the ice-free corridor could not have been the earliest route.

A study of the natural history, climate, and archaeology of the Sanak Island region off the coast of Alaska has concluded that the glaciers from the last Ice Age retreated from this island thousands of years earlier than scientists previously thought. Soil cores from the island contain pollen that proves that as many as 16,300 years ago, the island was dry and habitable. This means that although the corridor to North America was still blocked by ice, glaciers had retreated along the islands on the southern coast of Beringia. Prehistoric migrants could have paddled boats from island to island, fishing and hunting marine mammals as they made their way down the west coast of North and South America.

For centuries, the Inuit people of North America moved along coastal areas in animal-hide kayaks and lived off the bounty of the sea. Prehistoric people could have traveled the same way. A kelp-bed ecosystem runs from Japan, across to Alaska, and down the west coast of North and South America. Kelp supports seals, otters, sea urchins, and abalone, all foods that could have sustained prehistoric sailors. This theory lacks proof because, just as in Australia, there is no archaeological evidence of boats. However, scientists are trying to bolster the case of marine migrants with other data.

Sites on the Channel Islands off of California's southern coast reveal an island life that depended on the sea as many as 13,000 years ago. The middens on these islands prove that the inhabitants' diet included mussels, abalone, and black turban snails, along with crab, birds, and marine mammals. Prehistoric fish hooks were found in Daisy Cave on San Miguel Island.

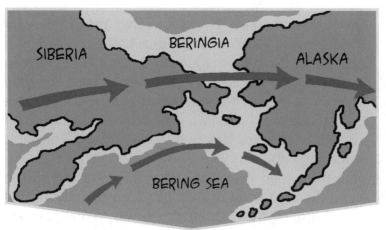

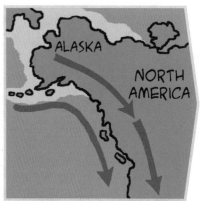

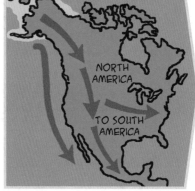

Clearly, the earliest migrants to America were very accustomed to life on the water. This bolsters the hypothesis that prehistoric people reached the New World by boat.

At any point on the coastal journey, migrants would have encountered America's vast network of rivers. People could have navigated these tributaries deep into the interior of the continent. In 2008, archaeologists from the University of Oregon discovered human excrement in a cave in central Oregon. This poop was between 15,000 and 14,000 years old, and it contained the seeds of desert parsley. This plant has roots that are hidden 1 foot below ground. People don't just stumble upon a plant like this. They have to know what they are looking for. This evidence suggests that humans had lived in the area for a while.

[It is more proof that humans arrived in North America much earlier than the Clovis culture, and probably moved inland from the West Coast.]

Geneticists are also trying to solve the mystery of American migration. Mitochondrial DNA extracted from a 10,300-year-old tooth found in On Your Knees Cave in Alaska was compared with genomes of modern Native Americans. The scientists who analyzed this data believe that people could not have migrated from Alaska down into North America before 16,500 years ago. They also found that the modern people most related to the prehistoric man who lost his tooth in Alaska still live along the west coast of the United States. They believe that this means prehistoric Americans migrated down the west coast and then eventually spread inland, developing more mutations as they traveled.

At this point, there are more questions than answers about exactly how and when the first migrants reached the Americas and where they came from. Clovis hunters did migrate from Asia and they established a sophisticated culture throughout North America, but they were not the first migrants to step foot on the continent. The mystery of American migration remains unsolved.

Our journey has brought us to every continent except Antarctica. That frozen place is reserved for modern explorers. But the story of human migration is not over. In many ways, it is just beginning.

KEY QUESTIONS

- Why did people believe the Clovis First theory for so long, even as evidence against it was found?
- What role did the climate play in early human's migration to the Americas?
- Why is an open mind important in the study of archaeology?

FOSSILIZED FECES

Scientists call fossilized feces coprolites. Find a friend and whip up separate batches of fake coprolites. Then exchange samples and see if you can make conclusions about your friend's environment based on his poop concoction. This recipe for fake coprolite makes one sample.

- **Decide on the region and time period you want your poop to showcase.** Do some research to discover what kind of food was present in which region during which time period. When did farming begin? What crops were native to what regions of the world? Decide on one or more mystery ingredients to add to your coprolite.

- **Follow the poop recipe.** Mix the poop to a smooth consistency.

- **Exchange your sample with your friend's.** Use a craft stick to dig through the sample. Keep a record of the evidence you find.

- **Draw conclusions from this evidence.** Where and when did this poop come from? What kind of environment did the person who made this poop live in? Talk to your friend. Were your conclusions correct?

> To investigate more, research the diets of modern people in different areas of the world. How does your diet compare with theirs? What does modern food reveal about our modern environment? What does it reveal about how migration has affected what we eat? Keep a record of what you eat for an entire day. What does this list of food reveal about your environment?

Ideas for Supplies

- mystery ingredients
- 2 cups flour
- 1 cup salt
- 2 tablespoons baking soda
- 2 tablespoons vegetable oil
- 1 cup hot water
- brown food coloring

Ideas for Supplies ▼

- Styrofoam or paper cups
- dirt and gravel
- clay
- a map of Beringia to use as a guideline

AN ICE AGE THAW

During the last Ice Age, much of North America was covered in a huge glacier. The movement of glaciers shaped our environment, creating lakes and valleys, depositing boulders, and eroding the land. Create a model of Beringia. Then see what happens when the climate of your model world grows warmer.

- **Fill several cups about half-full with a mixture of dirt and gravel.** Then fill with water and freeze overnight. These are your glaciers.

- **Using the Beringia map as a guideline and craft sticks as a tool, make a clay model of this landform on a cookie sheet.** Put the tray in the freezer to harden your map.

- **When your glaciers are frozen, remove them from the cups.** Simulate the movement of the glaciers by pressing the ice blocks across your Beringian landscape. Make them move as a glacier would creep, very slowly and in one direction, with a fair amount of pressure.

- **Record what happens to your landscape.** What impressions are made in the terrain? Does the glacier leave anything behind? Are there places in the landscape where the glacier made holes in the land?

- **Put what's left of your glaciers to each side of the land bridge and study them as they melt.** How is the sediment distributed in the glacial ice? Did the glaciers pick up any clay as they passed over the model? How might any picked-up material affect the glaciers' future flow? How is the sediment distributed as the ice melts?

- **How does this melting ice impact your model of the Beringia Land Bridge?** What happens if you suddenly heat up your environment by using a blow dryer to melt the ice quickly? Hypothesize how a warming trend would affect human migration from Asia to North America.

VOCAB LAB

Write down what you think each word means:

Beringia, coprolites, fertile, resources, scraper, symbolic behavior, hybrid, occipital bun, and **fertility**.

Compare your definitions with those of your friends or classmates. Did you all come up with the same meanings? Turn to the text and glossary if you need help.

To investigate more, research the different types of landforms glaciers create. Design an experiment similar to the one above in which you use ice and clay to make different landforms, such as cirques, striations, moraines, and drumlins. First, you will have to research what these landforms are and how glaciers shape them. Then, you will have to experiment with how large a chunk or sheet of ice you need.

Chapter Five
Expansion and Colonization

How did human migration change after the beginning of civilization?

WHAT ARE SOME OF THE THINGS THAT HELPED CIVILIZATION DEVELOP?

THE WHEEL.

AGRI-CULTURE.

DOMESTICATION OF ANIMALS.

THE ALPHABET.

GOOD! I THINK YOU ALL HAVE GOT IT!

UH, HELLO? YOU GUYS FORGOT TV, CANDY, AND VIDEO GAMES!

I GUESS I SPOKE TOO SOON.

We know more about the migration of people after humans began recording their experiences. Humans still migrated, but they met more people along the way and they often moved because of economic and political reasons.

Between 10,000 and 3500 BCE, the world was in the middle of a revolution. Humans learned how to farm. They domesticated animals. The invention of the alphabet made communication easier. The development of the wheel made transportation quicker. Nomads settled down, first in villages, which later swelled into cities. Cities became magnets for laborers, merchants, bureaucrats, and artisans. Trade flourished. Governments and religious institutions organized people into distinct groups with defined cultures. Civilization was born.

With civilization, migration took on a different look. People no longer moved through empty lands. More and more they encountered others as they traveled. Both the migrants and the hosts whose land they entered would be forever changed by these encounters.

BANTU MIGRATION: AFRICAN FARMERS ON THE MOVE

About 60,000 years ago, migration out of Africa started mankind's trek across the planet, but not everyone left their homeland. Those who remained formed the foundation for another great African migration, but this time people traveled within Africa. The Bantu people moved south and east across the continent in a slow migration that lasted hundreds of years, beginning in 3000 BCE.

The modern Bantu migration is unique for three reasons. First, the Bantu were not a single community or even one ethnic group. The word *Bantu* actually means "people," and it refers to Africans who speak one of the 500 languages that stem from a common parent tongue called Proto-Bantu.

> Today, there are about 90 million Bantu speakers in the world.

A second factor that makes the Bantu migration unusual was how long it lasted. While migrations in prehistoric times occurred during thousands of years, once civilization developed, most human migrations lasted only decades rather than millennia. This was not true for the Bantu. Around 3000 BCE, Bantu speakers began to move out of their homelands, which included the modern nations of Nigeria and Cameroon. By 1000 BCE, they occupied one-third of the continent. The duration of this 2,000-year-long migration makes it challenging for researchers to track.

WHAT DID YOU SAY?

Just as physical traits are passed on from one generation to the next, so is true language. Words are inherited from our ancestors and we pass them on to our offspring with minor changes. There are 500 languages and dialects that fall within the Bantu group. Here is the word for sun in four of those languages. Can you spot the similarities?

BANTU LANGUAGE	THE WORD FOR "SUN"
Neanga	azuba
Bemba	haka zuba
Chiwa	dzuba
Senga	zuba

TRAVEL TIPS

While a geneticist can follow migration patterns by tracking gene mutations, a linguist tracks mutations in language.

Finally, the Bantu people did not have a written language at the time they migrated, so there is no documentation of their journey. In a case such as this, linguists join the team of experts trying to piece together the story of this mass movement of people.

Languages that share similar vocabulary, grammar, and pronunciation probably came from the same mother tongue. Linguists group similar languages into a kind of family tree. Words contain clues to peoples' culture and religion, and words can hint at the geography of the place people lived in before they migrated.

> Linguists hunt for hidden meanings in words just as archaeologists dig for artifacts buried in sand.

Historians are not sure what started the Bantu migration 5,000 years ago, but two factors strengthened it—farming and iron-working. Africans began to farm about 8,000 years ago, when the climate was wet and the area now known as the Sahara Desert was full of game and fertile land. As the food supply increased, the population grew and more farmland was needed. However, by 6000 BCE, the desert was expanding and Bantu lands were drying up, so farmers picked up and moved east and south.

The Bantu migration did not move quickly, like an invading horde. Instead, small pockets of farmers moved to a new area, farmed for a while, and then moved on again.

As they moved, the Bantu used their iron hoes, picks, and axes to fell tropical forests. Logs from these trees helped fuel the fires artisans needed to smelt iron and forge more farming tools. As the Bantu began to farm more diverse crops, such as yams, sorghum, and millet, they needed to cultivate more land. Some farmers had to relocate again.

> Year after year, decade after decade, this process was repeated in a crisscross fashion across the African continent.

The lands the Bantu entered were not empty. The forests in the east were occupied by Bambuti, who hunted and gathered, while in the southwest region, the Khoi herded livestock in a savannah environment. In the path of the Bantu advance, the Bambuti either retreated deep into the forest or assimilated into Bantu communities. Although the Khoi were eventually outnumbered by Bantu, the new migrants learned animal husbandry from the people whose land they gobbled up. Southern Bantu words for milk, cow, and sheep all have Khoi origins.

RAIDERS AND TRADERS

When the Roman Empire collapsed in 476 CE, a dark age descended upon Western Europe. Cities disintegrated. Literacy almost vanished. Trade collapsed. Communities lived in isolation. Then, on a June morning in 793, that isolation ended.

The Viking long ships rode low in the water as they approached the island of Lindisfarne, England. Raiders lowered their sails and rowed silently so the monks in the monastery would not raise the alarm. The long boats drew up on the beach and the raiders raced across the sand. Fur-clad, helmeted Viking warriors poured over the monastery walls.

As the church bells called the monks to prayer, they were met with the ghastly sight of the Scandinavian raiders digging up and hauling away precious altars. They pillaged stores of food and stole all the gold and silver they could lay their hands on. Then the raiders either killed the monks or captured them to later be sold as slaves. After burning the monastery to the ground, the Vikings left as quickly as they came.

[
This raid at Lindisfarne marked
the beginning of the Viking Age,
which lasted until 1150.
]

The Vikings came from Scandinavia, a region that hangs like a dragon's head over Europe. Most Vikings eked out a living in small farming villages in that cold, harsh climate. People were organized into clans, and each clan had its own chief, who was usually the man with the biggest farm. When this leader wanted more land or goods, he led his tenant farmers and slaves on raids of neighboring villages.

In the late eighth century, political and environmental factors pushed the Vikings to expand from Scandinavia. Rival chiefs scrambling for power needed allies. They gave valuable gifts to men, bribing them in the quest to gain political and military power. When word spread that the Christian monasteries of Europe held riches, such as golden crucifixes and bejeweled goblets, ambitious chiefs decided that stealing from these distant lands would cement their power and prestige back home.

Once the Vikings gained tracts of land in the areas they'd attacked, many Scandinavians migrated to these regions. They went hoping for more space and a better life.

VIKINGS THEN & NOW

Much of what historians know about the Vikings has been learned from the Vikings' own stories. These sagas probably began as oral storytelling and were eventually written down in the tenth and eleventh centuries. You can still find plenty of evidence of Norse influence in today's culture, such as popular books by Rick Riordan and movies featuring the Norse god Thor. Go to the Icelandic Saga Database to read some epic adventures.

  Icelandic Saga Database

Viking naval technology was state of the art. They fashioned long ships from planks of oak that were overlapped and nailed together. Gaps between the boards were stuffed with tarred wool or animal hair to make them watertight. The lack of a keel made the ships easy to portage, and they could be sailed up shallow rivers. European communities that were far from the coast did not expect attacks from ocean pirates, so the Vikings had the advantage of surprise.

Eventually, the raiders set their sights on the rich cities of Europe. In 845, a Viking fleet of 120 ships sailed down the Seine River to Paris. The French king, Charles the Bald, surrendered before battle, paying the Viking chief 7,000 pounds of silver to go away. The Vikings took the money and proceeded upriver, where they wreaked havoc on other communities. The invaders decided to stay the winter in France. This gave them a quick launching off point for spring raiding. It also signaled the beginning of Viking assimilation into Europe.

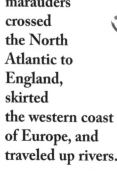

Viking marauders crossed the North Atlantic to England, skirted the western coast of Europe, and traveled up rivers.

BEHOLD! I'M A VIKING AND I'M HERE TO PLUNDER YOUR LUNCH!

OH, GREAT.

I'VE GOT A BETTER IDEA. HOW ABOUT I TRADE YOU TWO COOKIES FOR THAT SWORD?

I DO LOVE COOKIES...

HUH! I GUESS TRADING IS BETTER THAN PLUNDERING AFTER ALL.

What began as raids of plunder became a gradual migration that changed the face of Europe. When they wintered over in a region, the Vikings set up villages. They used locals as slaves to grind grain, wash laundry, and keep day-to-day life flowing smoothly. However, according to the Scandinavian system, slaves were given their freedom after several years. In this way, local people became citizens of these Viking communities. Slave women married Viking men and they raised children together. A hybrid culture of locals and Vikings gradually emerged in England, Ireland, Russia, and France.

The economy began to change, too. It became more profitable to make a living as a trader than a raider. Viking kings set up villages and established trading hubs in conquered areas, such as York in England, Dublin in Ireland, and Kiev in Ukraine. Viking merchants sold ivory, wheat, animal skins, and human slaves. They bought wine, weapons, silk, spices, and silver. Viking merchants traveled as far east as Constantinople and Jerusalem. The Norsemen became the hinge between the east and the west.

These interactions changed Viking culture both politically and religiously. The influx of trade goods and stolen silver made some leaders back in Scandinavia very wealthy. Smaller tribes began to unite under the protection of a single ruler, and these kingdoms eventually became the modern nations of Norway, Sweden, and Denmark.

The Vikings had been polytheistic, but Western Europe was Christian. This belief system slowly caught hold among the Scandinavians.

NEW MAPS

The Viking migration connected the world. Viking traders pioneered routes down the Volga River into Russia. They built trading towns in Ireland and settled islands around Scotland and England. They opened routes to Constantinople, the heart of the Byzantine Empire. Viking explorers settled Iceland and Greenland and were the first Europeans to reach the North American continent in 1000 CE.

When a Viking king converted to Christianity, all his subjects became Christian, too. It became unacceptable to raid communities of people who shared the same faith, and Viking raids ended as Christianity spread throughout Scandinavia.

FOR GOD AND MONEY: BRITISH COLONIZATION OF AMERICA

Advertisements today are full of glossy images and text designed to get us to buy certain products or act certain ways or believe certain ideas. These ads appeal to our dreams or play on our fears. Although they did not have shiny paper and digitally enhanced images, European companies in the seventeenth century used similar methods of persuasion to convince people to migrate to America.

Following the voyages of the explorer Christopher Columbus, the Spaniards gained the first foothold in the Americas. Conquistadors spread out across North and South America to "serve God and His Majesty . . . and to grow rich," as said by Bernal Díaz del Castillo, a Spanish conquistador. Great Britain was right on Spain's heels, determined not to let the prize of new land and resources slip through its hands.

Western Europe played by the rules of "finders keepers." The people who colonized unclaimed land got to develop it and reap its riches. Rich people were needed to put up the money that a colony required to get started, and people had to be willing to migrate to these unknown lands and build settlements.

A DEADLY HITCHHIKER

In the thirteenth century, Genghis Khan unified nomadic tribes in Mongolia and founded the largest land empire in the world. As Khan led massive armies across China, Korea, Central Asia, and Eastern Russia, a disease called the plague trailed his route. This lethal disease would kill an estimated 40 million people in China and eventually make its way to Europe, where two-thirds of the population would die in waves of infection that lasted for a century.

The first permanent British colony in North America was established in Jamestown, Virginia, in 1607. The Virginia Company was the group of investors who financed the Jamestown settlement. These merchants and bankers were betting that this colony would turn a profit and make them rich. However, by 1609, the company was short of money and migrants, so it posted an advertisement to attract both. The advertisement made Virginia sound like paradise: "The land yields naturally for the sustenance of man, abundance of fish, infinite store of deer, and hares, with many fruits." Who could resist such an opportunity?

The problem with this ad, and others like it, was that it did not tell the whole truth. The first hurdle migrants had to endure was the boat ride to America. People were packed below deck in bunks 2 feet across and 6 feet long. The ships carried 400 to 600 passengers, as well as equipment, provisions, and barrels of fresh water. The journey lasted between eight and twelve weeks. The air in the hold reeked of vomit, sweat, feces, and fear. People sickened from dysentery, seasickness, and scurvy.

Things grew worse once the migrants landed. The first years of the Jamestown colony were deadly. The winter of 1609–1610 is known as the Starving Time because out of 500 original settlers, only 60 colonists were alive when spring finally arrived. The settlers did not dare leave the fort to hunt for fear of being attacked by Powhatan warriors. They ate the leather from their boots, killed their horses and pets, and even cannibalized their dead.

No Fairy Tale

The story of Jamestown's founding has made its way into American popular culture. You might have heard of these characters: English Captain John Smith, Indian Chief Powhatan, Powhatan's daughter, the lovely Pocahontas. But children's stories and Disney movies only paint historical half-truths, and they leave out some of the most important players in the story.

Many of these early migrants were indentured servants. They were so poor back in England that the future held little prospect of a better life.

[
Indentured servants signed a contract agreeing to work as a servant for several years in exchange for their passage to America.
]

In 1623, an indentured servant named Richard Frethorne wrote to his family back in England and begged them to buy out the rest of his contract. "I have nothing to comfort me, nor there is nothing to be gotten here but sickness and death . . ." History is silent on his parents' reply.

Although supply ships from England did resupply the colony in the spring of 1610, life continued to be touch and go for years. From 1619 to 1623, the death rate at Jamestown hovered between 75 and 80 percent.

EYEWITNESS ACCOUNT

George Percy, the president of Jamestown colony during the Starving Time, wrote an account that records the challenges the early British migrants faced in this colony. Is this account different from ones you've previously heard?

 National Humanities Center Jamestown Percy relation

Despite the fact that so many British immigrants perished shortly after reaching America, people kept coming. By 1700, Great Britain had 14 colonies in North America and the English population was more than 400,000. These colonies would eventually become Canada and the United States.

Write down what you think each word means:

domesticate, **civilization**, **linguist**, **monastery**, **Scandinavia**, **tenant farmer**, **keel**, **polytheistic**, **conquistador**, and **colonize**.

Compare your definitions with those of your friends or classmates. Did you all come up with the same meanings? Turn to the text and glossary if you need help.

Migration was not just deadly for the migrants. A thriving population had already lived on the land for thousands of years when Europeans started arriving. No one knows for certain how many Native Americans lived in the Americas before Europeans arrived in the New World, but estimates range from a low of 1 million to a high of 112 million.

Archaeological and historical evidence suggests that the Native American population suffered dramatic declines following the migration of Europeans into the Americas. The Indians lacked immunities to European diseases, including smallpox, measles, and whooping cough. In some places, these illnesses wiped out 90 percent of the native population. Enslavement, war, and loss of land also decimated Indian people. When the first English settlers arrived in Jamestown, approximately 30,000 Algonquin Indians lived in the region. After years of sporadic warfare, only 2,000 Algonquin survived by the time they agreed to submit to English rule. This pattern was repeated by European colonizers throughout the Americas.

KEY QUESTIONS

- **Why is language an important part of the investigation of human migration?**
- **Why are there so many movies that depict characters and plots from Viking tales?**
- **Why wasn't the British government discouraged by the ongoing hardships at Jamestown?**

VIKING HEAD GEAR

Based on depictions in Viking artwork, historians believe that Viking soldiers wore round metal helmets into battle. However, a metal helmet would not offer much protection from the force of a heavy blow. Football helmets and modern soldiers' helmets are padded. How effectively does padding inside a helmet protect the brain? Design a padded helmet to find out. Note that this is a good investigation to do outside!

Ideas for Supplies ▼

- raw eggs to represent brains
- small containers to represent helmets
- different padding materials

- **Put a raw egg in a container.** Drop the container from a specific height. Does the egg break? If not, drop it from a greater height. Keep adjusting the height and record your results.

- **Repeat this procedure with other containers.** Add padding materials to protect your "brain." What do your results show about the best helmet design and the best padding to protect your egg?

- **A helmet must also be wearable in battle.** Is your helmet with the safest results a helmet that a soldier could wear on his head and still see and move around in? If not, how could you redesign the helmet and padding to make it more wearable?

photo credit: Markoz

> To investigate more, consider the fact that if you throw an egg across the room to another person and they catch it, the egg usually will not break. Why? Investigate the principles of potential and kinetic energy. How does your research contribute to your helmet design?

Ideas for Supplies ▼

- different types of food to test
- containers to store food

SOMETHING'S ROTTEN

When British colonists set sail for America, they not only packed food for the journey, but also for the first weeks following arrival. How did they bring food that would not rot quickly? They smoked, salted, and pickled much of the food they brought. What causes food to spoil? Test some common foods and decide what would go on your migration menu.

- **Put a sample of each food in two different storage environments.** For example, place a piece of pickle on a paper plate and in a canning jar.

- **Observe how the food changes over time.** This may take several days. Record changes in color, shape, and odor. How can you tell if the food is spoiled?

- **Which foods last the longest?** What conclusions can you make about why these foods hold up longer than others? Investigate the chemical properties of the different foods to help you answer these questions.

> To investigate more, try adding different ingredients to different foods, such as vegetable oil, water, and vinegar. How does this affect the length of time before the food begins to spoil? Do light and temperature have any affect on the food? What can you do to make different foods last longer?

Chapter Six
Oppression and Freedom

Why are some migrants forced to leave their homeland?

War, religious persecution, difficult economic conditions, natural disasters, and slavery are some of the reasons people are forced into migration.

Which has the power to motivate you more—fear or hope? Both emotions have moved people across continents. Dangerous and deadly conflicts, racial and ethnic discrimination, and large-scale natural disasters have forced people to leave their homes, many never to return. However, a hunger for religious, political, or economic freedom has also pulled migrants toward new lands and better lives.

THE JEWISH DIASPORA

Diaspora is a Greek word that means "to sow or scatter over a wide area." In ancient times, the Jewish people had a homeland in what is now known as Israel. During wars 2,000 years ago, the Jews were dispersed far and wide, not returning home again until the twentieth century. Religious intolerance is what forced the Jews from their homes.

> [Throughout history, migration
> has helped the Jews survive.]

The story of the first phase of Jewish migration lies at the root of the three monotheistic religions of the world—Judaism, Christianity, and Islam. All three faiths believe that around 2000 BCE, a man named Abraham lived in Ur, a city-state between the Tigris and Euphrates Rivers. According to sacred texts, he was the first man to pledge faith to one god and the first Jew. He traveled in search of Canaan, a land on the eastern Mediterranean that God had pledged to the Jewish people. From Canaan to Egypt and back again, the Jews moved repeatedly during many years. Finally, around 1000 BCE, they settled in their homeland with its capital at Jerusalem.

However, this land did not remain in Jewish hands for long. Ancient Near Eastern history is the story of one empire after another sweeping through the area, which is called the Fertile Crescent. Wars against the mighty Roman Empire in 70 CE and 132 CE brought great destruction and cast the Jews far and wide. The nation of Israel disappeared. Many Jewish people were killed, sold into slavery, or banished. This scattering is known as the Great Diaspora.

During times of crisis, Christian Europe became increasingly anti-Semitic. The word *Semitic* refers to Jewish people. So *anti-Semitic* means "anti-Jewish." Forced to wear distinctive clothing or live in walled-off areas of the city known as ghettos, Jews lived as second-class citizens. Despite this discrimination, many Jewish people still managed to become successful merchants, bankers, and professionals. Millions more immigrated to the United States for both economic reasons and to escape religious discrimination.

TRAVEL TIPS

The Fertile Crescent is an area in the Middle East that is bordered by water and high mountains, all of which creates a temperate climate suitable for growing crops.

Powerless and persecuted for their religious beliefs, Jews settled in communities around the globe.

Then, in 1914, World War I began, and Jewish communities in Europe were hit hard. Russian authorities drove Jews into the interior of the country. In Ukraine, at least 60,000 Jews were victims of pogroms, which today is called ethnic cleansing. The German army pressed Jews into labor gangs.

World governments attempted to find a place Jews could call their own. The British government issued the Balfour Declaration, which was a commitment to create a Jewish homeland by carving up the Arab nation of Palestine. This territory had once been the ancient land of Canaan, which Jews still believed was their God-given homeland. But before this Jewish state could be formed, Europe geared up for the Second World War.

In the 1930s, Adolf Hitler led the Nazi party to power in Germany. As anti-Semitism became national policy, Jews were stripped of their German citizenship and forced to wear yellow stars on their clothing. Banned from schools and with their businesses destroyed, Jews were segregated in their ghettos, where hunger and disease stalked them.

The rest of the world knew how brutal the Nazi regime was, but other nations did little to save the Nazis' Jewish victims. In 1938, a conference was held by 32 nations, but each was willing to accept only a few Jewish refugees.

[
The Jews were desperate to escape the Nazi regime, but no one wanted them. Then, it was too late.
]

In 1939, Germany invaded Poland and World War II began. Soon, migration routes were cut off and the extermination of the Jews became the official policy of Germany.

After World War I, anti-Semitism grew in Great Britain, Canada, and the United States. These nations severely restricted the number of Jewish immigrants they would allow into their countries, so Jews relocated to places such as Shanghai, Brazil, and Mexico.

By the war's end, more than 6 million Jews from countries throughout Europe had been murdered in gas chambers and death camps. History has labeled this genocide as the Holocaust.

After World War II ended in 1945, Jewish survivors were caught in a state of homelessness. Many nations still did not want them. Jews tried to migrate to the land that had been committed to them by the Balfour Declaration, but they were violently turned away by the British. Some were smuggled in anyway, and Jewish resistance against British authorities began. The British finally turned over the question of a Jewish state to the United Nations.

In 1947, the United Nations recommended that Palestine be partitioned into separate Jewish and Arab states. On May 14, 1948, the state of Israel was born, and in 1950, the Israeli government declared the Law of Return. This law allowed Jewish people from anywhere in the world to migrate to Israel. Jews, many of them refugees and death camp survivors from war-torn Europe, migrated by the hundreds of thousands. The people of the Great Diaspora were finally home after 2,000 years.

However, peace was not to be. Palestinian Arabs refused to relinquish land they had been living on for centuries without a fight. Immediately after Israel declared its statehood, Palestinian rebels and the armies of nearby Arab countries attacked Israel. The Arabs lost. With the cease-fire agreement, Israel gained approximately 75 percent of Palestinian land. Hundreds of thousands of Palestinians were forced to move into refugee camps in neighboring countries. Decades of war followed, and this conflict remains ongoing. Today, there are 5 million Palestinian refugees. Approximately 1.5 million of them live in overcrowded camps with poor water and sewer facilities and high unemployment.

REMAINING CONNECTED

Evidence of centuries of diasporas can be seen in communities of Jewish people around the world. In Myanmar, a 100-year-old synagogue is open for daily worship. A few hundred Jews on the island nation of Tahiti fly kosher food in from the United States and Australia.

In Cuba, a nation with a communist government that spent many years in political isolation, Jews freely practice their religion. The religion of Judaism is the force that has maintained the link between these scattered migrants. Traditional prayers, marrying within the faith, following dietary laws, a shared history of persecution—these experiences create bonds that connect Jews all over the world.

THE SLAVE TRADE

The largest forced migration in history lasted almost 400 years. Between 1500 and the 1850s, at least 12 million free people were captured in the interior of Africa. Many countries, including Portugal, Britain, France, Spain, and the Dutch Empire, participated in the slave trade that brought slaves to the New World.

After being captured, the prisoners were forced to walk hundreds of miles to slave forts along the coast, where they were traded for rum, cloth, and guns. They might be kept in these forts, under deplorable conditions, for as long as three months before being loaded into slave ships.

[Slaves were shackled and crammed, spoon-like, into the bowels of slave ships.]

They endured a hellish transport across the Atlantic Ocean. Called the Middle Passage, the journey lasted 60 to 90 days. Between 10 and 15 percent of the slaves died at sea before ever seeing land again.

Once the ships reached the Caribbean, the Africans were auctioned off at slave markets and went to work in homes and plantations across North and South America. The Africans and any children born to them were considered the property of the slave owners. They had no rights, no freedom, and no hope.

While some groups had always been vocal about the moral and social ills of slavery, countries didn't begin to officially end the practice until the late 1700s. It wasn't until after the mid-1800s that slavery was finally abolished completely. The repercussions of this dark period in human history persist even today.

GREAT MIGRATION OF AFRICAN-AMERICANS

Between 1910 and 1930, one-tenth of African-Americans who lived in the southern United States moved north. They wanted to escape racism and find better economic opportunities. The Schomburg Center for Research in Black Culture has an interactive website that showcases how this mass migration changed the face of the American urban landscape.

  Great Migration in motion

MIGRATION FORCED BY WAR

One out of every 122 people in the world is an involuntary migrant. If these people were grouped into one area, they would make up the 24th largest country in the world. In the spring of 2015, the United Nations high commissioner for refugees reported that nearly 60 million people had been displaced from their homes during 2014. This is the highest number of forcibly displaced people that has ever been recorded in one year.

Muhannad and Nasser are two of these modern migrants. These men are from Syria, a nation that erupted into civil war in 2011. Approximately 200,000 civilians have died in this conflict and at least another 11 million have been forced from their homes. More than 4 million Syrians have fled the country to neighboring Turkey, Jordan, and Lebanon.

Nasser and Muhannad have been friends since college. The war in Syria interrupted their career plans. After spending years in limbo in Lebanon and Turkey, the two men decided to take their chances and seek a better life in Europe.

World War II, which lasted from 1939 to 1945, proved that man could slaughter man at inconceivable levels. Approximately 50 million people died in this global conflict. Fields and cities were demolished and millions of people were displaced. At the end of the war, many people could not return home. Political leaders had redrawn national borders and, in some cases, the country people had called home was now a different nation.

ROHINGYA MUSLIM REFUGEES

The Rohingya are a Muslim minority living in the Buddhist nation of Myanmar. They have long been discriminated against because of their religion. Myanmar refuses to give citizenship rights to the Rohingya, and they are often victims of violence and discrimination. In the spring of 2015, many Rohingya fled Myanmar on the boats of smugglers, seeking sanctuary in other countries. However, neighboring countries did not want them and the ships were often turned away. *The New York Times* ran a photo essay about the desperate plight of these migrants.

 New York Times lens rohingya refugee

When asked what they were looking for as they began this dangerous migration, Nasser replied, "Safety, a job, and a good life. We don't want anything else."

Their journey was perilous. They found a smuggler on Facebook and paid him $1,000 each to ferry them across the Aegean Sea from Turkey to Greece. The men waited anxiously at the designated spot for the signal that their journey was to begin. One morning, the smuggler gave the go-ahead. Muhannad and Nasser pulled on their life jackets and climbed aboard a rubber dinghy, their cell phones wrapped in layers of plastic baggies. Forty-three people, including a small child, piled into the rubber boat alongside Nasser and Muhannad.

After two hours, they neared land. Suddenly, a Greek coast guard vessel approached. The smuggler plunged a knife into the dinghy, ensuring that the guards could not force the migrants to sail back into Turkish waters. Luckily, all the passengers made it to shore.

> Many are not so fortunate. From January to August of 2015, more than 2,000 migrants drowned trying to cross the Mediterranean Sea.

Nasser and Muhannad unwrapped their cell phones and checked their GPS to find their location. Elated that they had reached Greece, they took selfies to celebrate. Then, they began to walk. They planned to trek through Macedonia, Serbia, and Hungary to reach the nations of northern Europe where jobs are more plentiful and there is assistance for immigrants.

The status of migrants such as Muhannad and Nasser is controversial. Are they immigrants or refugees? The distinction is important. An immigrant *chooses* to move to another country. A refugee is *forced* to leave.

Nations have legal processes by which immigrants are allowed to reside in a country and eventually gain citizenship. But if a person enters a country without going through those legal hoops, they are considered undocumented aliens and can be deported. A refugee can apply for asylum. To gain this protected status, a refugee has to be able to demonstrate that if he returned home, he would be injured or killed because of his race, religion, nationality, or politics.

[
That can be very hard to prove, especially for people such as Nasser and Muhannad, who flee with little more than the clothes on their backs.
]

The two men trudged through mud, forded streams, and snuck past police as they walked through Macedonia, Serbia, and Hungary. By the time they arrived in Germany, they had traveled more than 1,553 miles by boat, train, bus, car, and foot.

The pair had planned to go on to Luxembourg or the Netherlands, but suddenly a policeman came up to them. He offered them fruit and said that they needed to accompany him to the police station to apply for asylum. The kindness with which the officials in the small border town treated Muhannad and Nasser convinced them to remain in Germany. They are being sheltered at an asylum center while their applications for refugee status are processed.

TRAVEL TIPS

Prehistoric migrants used chipped and flaked stone tools to survive on their global trek. Modern migrants rely on smartphones. Traffickers advertise their services on social media. Migrants use GPS to find key locations, and they communicate on Twitter and Facebook with other travelers about safe routes and conditions. Osama Aljasem, a music teacher from Syria, said, "I would never have been able to arrive at my destination without my smartphone. I get stressed out when the battery even starts to get low."

VOLUNTARY MIGRATION

Have you ever visited the Statute of Liberty in New York Harbor? This famous robed figure holds a torch in her uplifted hand and a broken chain lies at her feet. Since the 1880s, the Statute of Liberty has represented the spirit of immigrants—a desire for freedom.

Throughout history, people have moved in search of economic freedom. They want to make more money, buy a home, and provide their children with opportunities that they did not have. For much of the nineteenth and twentieth centuries, the United States represented such a dream destination. From 1815 to 1915, millions of Europeans and tens of thousands of Asians came in search of cheap land and job opportunities in the growing industrial economy that was developing in the United States at that time.

> A poem by Emma Lazarus is inscribed on the base of the Statute of Liberty: "Give me your tired, your poor, your huddled masses yearning to breathe free . . . ."

In fact, the immigrants who arrived in the United States during this century of migration were not the poorest of the poor. They were ambitious, skilled, and often educated. These migrants paid their own way to the United States or were funded by relatives or recruited by companies seeking laborers.

The major port of entry for migrants crossing the Atlantic Ocean was Ellis Island in New York. Officials inspected the migrants' eyes, ears, and lungs, searching for infectious diseases. They were interrogated on their religious and political views.

ACROSS AMERICA

State-to-state migration can affect the politics and economy of the United States. Where were you born? Have you stayed in that state? Do you think your future is in your home state? Take a look at these charts to see where people are moving to and from within America.

New York Times where people were born

Economic migrations are sparked when people hear of a destination where work is available.

> If the travelers passed these checkpoints, they took an oath of loyalty to the United States and were allowed to enter the nation.

GOLD MOUNTAIN

Not all people who migrated to the United States in the nineteenth century entered through Ellis Island. Chinese immigrants arrived on the West Coast and were processed at Angel Island in San Francisco Bay. Tales of gold lured them to a continent far from home, but instead of riches, they often found racism.

Lee Chew recounted his experience in *The Biography of a Chinaman*, published in 1903. Forty years earlier, his father gave him $100, and Chew and five boys from his village sailed on a ship to the United States.

When Chew arrived in San Francisco, he did not dig for gold. Instead, he found work as a servant for a white family, the kind of work many Chinese men were forced to take.

An immigration interview on Angel Island in the 1920s

photo credit: National Archives

TRACE YOUR TREE

Today, Ellis Island is a national park where you can visit the National Museum of Immigration. The Ellis Island Foundation also maintains a database of the 51 million people who came through Ellis Island from 1892 through 1954. You can look up your own ancestors. Do you find anything surprising? Talk to your family to see if you can learn more about immigrants in your family.

 liberty Ellis passenger

After two years, Chew and a partner moved inland to where the transcontinental railroad was being laid. They opened up a laundry business, worked hard, and saved their profits. Eventually, Chew moved to New York and opened up his own store in the Chinese section of the city. His story is typical of Chinese immigrants to the United States at the turn of the twentieth century.

[
They worked hard, sent money back
to China, and slowly prospered.
]

However, too often in history, migrants whose labor is desired in good times are resented when the economy turns bad. When the United States fell into an economic depression in 1873, the Chinese became scapegoats. Labor unions claimed that Chinese men were taking jobs away from Americans because they worked for less money. In 1882, the Chinese Exclusion Act barred almost all Chinese from entering the United States. The law also declared that Chinese immigrants could never become citizens. The Chinese Exclusion Act remained law until 1943.

TRAVEL TIPS

In 1848, the year that gold was discovered in California, only 50 Chinese people lived there. By 1852, at least 25,000 Chinese had immigrated to the United States, and that number swelled to more than 300,000 by 1882.

WHAT ARE YOU DOING?

RESEARCHING THE CHINESE IMMIGRANT EXPERIENCE.

DID YOU KNOW THAT FOR 50 YEARS, AMERICA BLOCKED ALMOST ALL CHINESE IMMIGRATION?

AND CHINESE IMMIGRANTS COULDN'T BECOME U.S. CITIZENS?

WHAT?! THAT'S...THAT'S... UNAMERICAN!

Lee Chew expressed the frustration that many Chinese migrants felt at the unfairness they faced in their new homeland: "More than half the Chinese in this country would become citizens if allowed to do so, and would be patriotic Americans. But how can they make this country their home as matters now are?"

Chinese immigrants who managed to enter the United States before the exclusion law went into effect were discriminated against in many ways. They were not allowed to testify against white people in court. They had to pay special "alien" taxes. They were prohibited from marrying white people and were banned from sections of certain cities.

The Chinese fought back. They filed lawsuits against the Exclusion Act, invoking the Fourteenth Amendment, which grants citizenship rights to anyone born in the United States. After 1943, only 105 Chinese people were allowed to migrate to the United States each year. So many Chinese entered the country illegally that, in 1950, the government offered amnesty to all unregistered Chinese and 20,000 came to register. The discriminatory quotas that unfairly restricted Chinese immigration to the United States were finally abolished in 1965.

BRACERO PROGRAM

The word *bracero* means manual laborer in Spanish. From 1942 to 1964, the United States contracted with the Mexican government to allow more than 4.5 million Mexican guest workers to temporarily migrate to the United States to work as farm laborers. These laborers were often poorly paid and worked in dangerous conditions. Photos of the braceros' experience can be seen in an online exhibit by the National Museum of American History.

American
move
bracero

KEY QUESTIONS

- Do the countries that captured free men and enslaved them have any obligation to the communities they disrupted hundreds of years ago?

- Why do nations close their borders to certain groups of people?

- Can you find more examples of forced migration occurring today? What can you do to help?

From 1910 to 1940, Angel Island in San Francisco Bay served as the immigration processing station for migrants entering the United States from Asia. Because of the Chinese Exclusion Act of 1882, any Chinese who migrated could be detained for months or even years before being either released or deported. The detainees wrote poetry on the walls of their cells that reveals their despair and hope. You can read the poems and listen to the experiences of Chinese immigrants. What do they make you think of? Can you think of other times in history when similar events occurred?

PS

🔎 Poetic Waves

MIGRATION POETRY

A migrant who is forced to leave home will have an experience different from a migrant who chooses to leave home. A migrant who intends to remain in his host country forever will have emotions different from a migrant who wants to make money and return home as quickly as possible. Research the experiences of forced and voluntary migrants from different times in history. Create a "wall" of poetry that communicates what you imagine these individuals felt about their journeys.

- **With an adult's permission, use the Internet to research the experiences of forced and voluntary immigrants. Consider including the following groups.**

  - Irish during the potato famine

  - Great Migration of African-Americans

  - Cherokee Trail of Tears

  - Rohingya Muslims fleeing Myanmar

  - British deportation of criminals to Australia

  - Vietnamese boat people

  - Muslims and Hindus when India was partitioned

  - Armenian deportation by Turks

  - Lost Boys of Sudan

- **Create a free-verse poem.** It should be based on your understanding of what this experience of migration would have been like for the group you researched. Paint or carve this poem on your own "wall."

To investigate more, listen to some reggae songs. These songs often refer to the lasting effects of slavery. They originate out of the Rastafari movement of Jamaica, which works to ensure that history is not forgotten. Try to write lyrics to your own reggae song. How is this different from writing poetry? How is writing poetry similar?

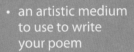

Ideas for Supplies ▼

- an artistic medium to use to write your poem
- printer ink
- something to use as your wall—banner paper, poster paper, Styrofoam, wood

VOCAB LAB

Write down what you think each word means:

Judaism, monotheism, Fertile Crescent, ethnic cleansing, kosher, communist, refugee, and **deport.**

Compare your definitions with those of your friends or classmates. Did you all come up with the same meanings? Turn to the text and glossary if you need help.

Diagram of a slave ship

Detail

To investigate more, compare the mortality rates on ships from different countries. What factors might make one nation's slave ships less deadly than another's? How did mortality rates change over time? Why?

THE MATHEMATICS OF MORTALITY: THE TRIANGLE SLAVE TRADE

Use math to analyze the human toll slavery exacted on millions of African people. Research slave voyages by using data found on the website Trans-Atlantic Slave Trade Database.

Trans-Atlantic slave database

- **With an adult's permission, use the Internet to study historical blueprints and artistic images of conditions on the slave ships.** Read historical accounts from ship captains and doctors.

- **Design math problems to explore the mortality rate of slaves during the Middle Passage.** The mortality rate is found by taking the number of slaves who died on a voyage, divided by the number of people who boarded the ship, multiplied by 100. Consider how these factors influenced the mortality rate.

  - amount of time a ship spent on the African coast
  - length of voyage
  - number of slaves on board
  - type and size of ship
  - gender and age of slaves

- **How can you plot this data?** Can you plot it in such a way that it educates other people about the human toll of this era of forced migration?

Chapter Seven ▶
The Future of Human Migration

How will the earth's
populations change
in the future?

People will continue to migrate for economic and environmental reasons and will change the cities and towns of the world for both better and worse.

For hundreds of years, life in the Chinese village of Liu Gong changed very little. Farmers in this community of 70 people grew wheat and corn. Life was hard and famine struck every few years. In the 1990s, the Chinese government began to experiment with economic reforms, and the nearby city of Chongqing became a place of investment and opportunity. As a result, the tiny village of Liu Gong was transformed.

Farmland became forests of apartment buildings cascading down hillsides. Today, electrical and cable wires create spiderwebs above streets. Raw sewage spills into open gutters. Vehicles clog what used to be a footpath. The population of Liu Gong quickly grew from 70 people to 10,000 and then exploded to 120,000 as the village fused with neighboring towns surrounding Chongqing, which is now a metropolis of 10 million. The migration of people to Liu Gong shows no sign of slowing.

Mr. Wang saved up for two years to move to Liu Gong, where he rents a small shop and builds traditional Chinese bathtubs. His family lives in a windowless room in the back of the shop. Wang believes moving to Liu Gong was the right decision: "Here, you can turn your grandchildren into successful people if you find the right way to make a living—in the village you can only live." Wang represents the face of the future of human migration.

> Global economic forces, the growing population of young people, and climate change will result in large-scale migration in the twenty-first century.

THE ECONOMICS OF MIGRATION

Economic opportunities have inspired migration throughout history and will continue to do so in the future. Since the end of World War II, international trade laws and world governing bodies have reduced barriers to trade. That makes it easier for companies to transfer goods and invest money around the world.

This globalization process has created pockets of wealth and opportunity, and people are migrating to follow the money. A worker from Yemen will earn 15 times more money in the United States than he would in Yemen, simply because the United States has a richer economy. A worker from Mexico will earn two and a half times more money in the United States than in Mexico. Money will continue to be an incentive for people to migrant in the future.

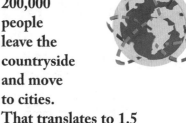

Every day, 200,000 people leave the countryside and move to cities. That translates to 1.5 million rural-to-urban migrants a week and 70 million a year.

Still, it costs money to move. Historically, this has meant that the very poorest people in the world did not migrate. If someone can barely afford to eat, how can they buy a bus or boat or airplane ticket and start life over in a new country? However, the poverty rate is declining. In 1983, the number of people who lived on less than $1.25 a day was 43 percent of the world's population. Today, the extreme poor make up about 15 percent.

Being less poor means people have a better chance to migrate where jobs are located. Nations in the Middle East and sub-Saharan Africa have the lowest wages in the world, so, in the future, these are the places from which migrants will come as extreme poverty continues to decline.

Economic development means that urban areas will be magnets for migration in the twenty-first century, especially in the developing world. History has shown that as a country develops, people move from rural areas into the city. In 2008, 50 percent of the world's population still lived in villages, most of these in Asia and Africa. By 2050, another 3.1 billion people will have moved to urban areas, and by the end of this century, more than three-quarters of the world's population will live in cities.

The age of the world's population will also impact the future of migration. The poorest countries have the highest birth rates. For example, the population of sub-Saharan Africa is expected to grow by 1 billion people by 2050. These young people will be more educated than people in past generations. By 2050, more than 70 percent of the world's youth will have finished primary school, and the number of students with college degrees in sub-Saharan Africa will double.

This means there will be greater numbers of youth in the poorest countries in the world, and these young people will have schooling and skills. If they move into an urban area in their own country and cannot find a job, their frustration will grow. A mass of educated, unemployed, and frustrated youth crowded into a megacity is a recipe for violence and political unrest.

> Migration will be a safety valve for poor countries.

CLIMATE CHANGE MIGRATION

Mother Nature will be another cause of migration in the future. Climate change predictions for our planet are frightening, and include mega-storms, vanishing forests, oceans empty of fish, infertile farmland, desertification, and rising seas. The term "environmental refugee" has been used to refer to people who are forced to migrate due to environmental changes.

The Intergovernmental Panel on Climate Change predicts that within a decade, at least 270 million people in Latin America, Asia, and Africa will not have enough water. By the middle of the twenty-first century, another 130 million Asians will be at risk of hunger due to the changing climate. By the year 2100, the amount of money that Africans earn from the sale of crops will have dropped by 90 percent.

These conditions might force people to move, and this migration will be unlike any the world has seen. The world's most vulnerable people will be migrating to places already crammed full of vulnerable people. Gaurpodomando, a Bangladeshi fisherman, has been struggling to remain in his village as declining fish populations, flooding, and cyclones make life almost impossible. Most of the men in his family have already migrated to Indian cities to find work. But Gaurpodomando does not want to move.

> ["I don't want to leave this country," he said. "I love this place." Soon, he might not have a choice.]

Sometimes, after a sudden catastrophe, people return home and rebuild. Hurricane Katrina tore through the Gulf Coast in 2005, displacing 1.5 million people. However, within three months, approximately 90 percent of those migrants had returned to the county they lived in when the storm struck.

What happens to people who cannot afford to rebuild after a disaster or whose ability to make a living is crippled by the consequences of climate change? They become permanent environmental refugees.

THE SINKING MALDIVES

Malé is the capital of Maldives, an archipelago nation composed of 1,200 tiny islands in the Pacific. Malé is an urban island, heavily fortified with man-made sea walls, harbors, and artificial beaches. The island lacks natural reef and sediment protection against rising sea levels. Political leaders and scientists fear that if something is not done to slow the rising sea levels, Malé, and other urban islands, will disappear beneath the ocean forever.

After one flood too many, Mohammad Ayub Ali gave up farming in his village in central Bangladesh. He moved to Dhaka, where he now drives a rickshaw. Ali makes $15 a month and lives in a slum with his mother, wife, two children, and 3.5 million poor people, including many environmental refugees just like him.

IMPACTS OF FUTURE MIGRATION

Human migration poses both challenges and opportunities. Cities are under pressure as masses of migrants flood their borders. Political leaders try to balance public opinion, international pressure, and economic realities. However, despite the complex problems migration presents, the movement of humans across borders is inevitable and results in a vibrant global culture that can enrich everyone's lives.

Life in a big city has many advantages. There are more jobs and educational opportunities. Health care is more accessible. If a city is planned properly, land and energy can be used more efficiently than in rural areas, where people are spread far apart. However, the pace of migration at present poses threats for urban life in the future.

Cities are growing too big. By 2025, at least 27 cities will have populations of at least 10 million, and another 600 cities will have 1 million residents or more. Many of these megacities will be located in underdeveloped nations, including Lagos, Nigeria; Karachi, Pakistan; and Dhaka, Bangladesh.

The impact that climate change has on future migration depends on what governments do to deal with environmental threats.

TRAVEL TIPS

Today, one out of every six urban dwellers breathes polluted air. One out of every 15 people has inadequate sanitation facilities, and one out of 30 does not have access to safe drinking water.

Rising birth rates and migration have caused the populations in these cities to explode. Governments have not been able to manage the challenges posed by so many people living so closely together.

Cities are not just growing too big, they are also growing too quickly. The population of London grew seven-fold during the entire nineteenth century. In contrast, the population of Dhaka exploded more than 5,400 times between 1950 and 2015. City administrators cannot build enough apartment buildings, subways, sewers, hospitals, and schools to keep pace with the rising populations. For example, in Mumbai, India, transit trains were built with nine cars to hold a total of 2,628 passengers. Today, during rush hour, 4,500 people ride each train.

> Industries draw these migrants to the cities, but as industry grows, the quality of life deteriorates.

Chinese cities experienced an industrial boom during the beginning of this century, but the factories and power plants have brought air pollution along with employment. About 500,000 Chinese die each year from causes related to the severe air pollution.

As cities burst at the seams, migrants begin to look outside of their own countries for better lives. This causes international tensions. India is building a wall to keep out illegal immigrants from Bangladesh. As Italy rescues North African migrants from the Mediterranean Sea, Italian leaders express resentment at other European Union countries, which they claim do not do their fair share to aid refugees fleeing war and poverty. Political leaders have great influence over the tone of debate about migration and the solutions proposed to the problems it poses.

THE ROLE OF GOVERNMENT

As urban migration fills cities to their breaking points, mayors and city administrators are taking the lead to improve the quality of life for their residents. In the 1980s, the Chinese city of Shenzhen had about 300,000 people. Today, it has 15 million. To deal with the dangerous levels of air pollution caused by such rapid development, Shenzhen became the first Chinese city to create a carbon marketplace.

In 2013, the city put a cap on the amount of carbon dioxide emissions a manufacturer can emit into the atmosphere. Companies must either reduce pollution levels or buy carbon credits from another company that produces emissions below the cap. This program creates economic incentives to conserve energy and to use clean coal technology.

National leaders are taking the lead to improve cities in India. Prime Minister Narendra Modi plans to build 100 "smart" cities by 2022. While some of these will be brand-new urban areas, ancient cities will also be radically remodeled. Digital grids will connect sewage, electrical, communication, and transportation systems in these high-tech communities.

TRAVEL TIPS

The carbon marketplace in Shenzhen resulted in a significant drop in CO_2 emissions for the city. The practice of using a carbon marketplace has expanded to other Chinese cities as well.

THE SMART CITY OF THE FUTURE.
SOLAR PANELS
ENVIRONMENT-FRIENDLY SMART BUILDINGS
SMART HOUSING
WIND FARM
INTELLIGENT TRANSPORTATION SYSTEM

IT'S SO COOL! I WANT TO GO LIVE THERE NOW!
ME, TOO!

REPLACEMENT MIGRATION

Some European countries are debating the idea of replacement migration. This is a controversial idea that calls for allowing enough migrants into a country to maintain the balance between the working population and the non-working population. To keep this ratio even, Europe would need to allow 1.3 billion people to migrate by 2050.

TRAVEL TIPS

When there are more elderly people than young people in a country, health care and pension benefits must be cut. The quality of life for the older generation suffers. That is the situation facing a number of developed nations today.

[Currently, 350 million Indians live in cities, and by 2030, that number will rise to 600 million.]

Amjer is an ancient Indian city of 550,000 people. Currently, running water is available only a couple of hours every two days. Only two traffic lights work and sewage spills into the streets from houses not connected to the waste system. Some Indians doubt whether such a decrepit infrastructure can be updated without bankrupting the country. However, the prime minister's vision is important. It demonstrates that political leaders finally recognize that India's future depends on improving urban areas.

DEVELOPED COUNTRIES NEED MIGRANTS

Migration from developing countries offers a solution for the labor needs of wealthier countries. Overall, the world population rate continues to rise at a rate of 1.2 percent a year. However, there are countries that are actually shrinking. For example, by 2060, more than 40 percent of Japan's population will be over age 65. If these developed nations want to maintain their economies, they need to put out the welcome mat for migrants.

When people reach retirement age, they leave the workforce. The workers of the country support these retired individuals. But when there are more retired people than workers, not enough people pay taxes to support government programs.

A country needs a birthrate of 2.1 children per woman in order to sustain its given population in the future. The birthrate in many developed countries is below the replacement rate.

While the replacement model makes economic sense, it is often politics that controls who is allowed into a country. Developed countries prefer the best and the brightest migrants. However, labor shortages exist in low-skilled jobs as well as high. Countries that understand this and make migration easier often reap economic gains. For example, since 2003, the percent of Africans migrating to the Chinese city of Guangzhou has grown between 30 and 40 percent per year. Connections between the migrants' home communities and their host city is fueling trade between China and the vast African continent.

Another example of the importance of future migration to a nation's economic growth is in the high-tech field. The United States tightened migration at the turn of the twenty-first century, making it more difficult for Indians who work in information technology (IT) to move to Silicon Valley.

In the United States, the birthrate is about 1.88 births per woman. Germany, Spain, and Italy are all at 1.4, while Japan, Korea, and Eastern European countries are at about 1.3 births per woman.

India invested in its own IT industry, which grew eight-fold between 1994 and 2001. The United States missed out on the economic potential that these migrants could have provided to a growing industry.

MELTING POT OR SALAD BOWL?

Migration can be positive or negative for a community, and immigrants can be absorbed into their new homes in different ways. Two metaphors represent different ways to incorporate migrants into a society—the melting pot and the salad bowl.

The melting pot model expects immigrants to assimilate or blend in. They are expected to speak the language of the host country and accept its values and norms as their own. In contrast, the salad bowl model aims at creating a multicultural society, one that recognizes distinct cultural and ethnic differences within a nation.

Even if a country enacts policies to achieve a melting pot culture, migration inevitably changes the host community. Nations around the world are becoming more diverse.

DO YOU SPEAK SPANGLISH?

Many Latin American immigrants to the United States speak Spanglish, a blend of English and Spanish. A person may switch from one language to the next while blending words together into new hybrids.

Spanglish: parquear

Spanish: estacionar

English: to park

Spanglish: ¿Estás ready?

Spanish: ¿Estás listo?

English: Are you ready?

Half of the world's countries have an official language, but this is not always the language most commonly spoken. For example, Irish Gaelic is the first official language of Ireland, but only about 5 percent of the population uses it regularly. The Irish mainly speak English, the language that migrants brought to the island centuries ago.

Migration in the future will cause conflict. Scarce resources will fuel competition between natives and newcomers. Religious, political, and social customs will clash. However, culture is dynamic. In the future, as in the past, migrants and natives will encounter each other in schools and workplaces and churches and mosques. They will have conversations, share food, and eventually some will marry. New identities will be formed, and a rich, vibrant, global culture will continue to evolve.

The movement of people across the planet will ebb and flow, but it will never end. Everyone on the planet shares a heritage with those first people who arose in Africa 200,000 years ago. The urge to move is in our DNA. Migration is part of what it means to be human.

TRAVEL TIPS

Those jeans you are wearing were created by a German immigrant, Levi Strauss. That salsa beat in the song you are listening to originated in Cuba. And that chicken curry you are eating was brought by migrants from South Asia.

In reality, human migration is never so clear as a melting pot or a salad bowl. A better metaphor shows that in most countries, migrants and natives merge together in a kind of soupy salad that at times tastes very bitter, but at other times is deliciously sweet.

KEY QUESTIONS

- Why are migrants attracted to cities instead of rural areas? How does an influx of migrants affect the urban areas of a country?

- Migration is both a personal journey and a global one. How does the media explore these two dynamics?

Ideas for Supplies ▼

- sand
- clean plastic tubs, such as dishpans or cat litter box
- large block of wood and several small blocks of wood

NO DAY AT THE BEACH

Wind, waves, and water all shape the earth's beaches. Sand erosion and accretion occur naturally, but can also be influenced by human behavior, such as damning rivers, building structures along the coast, and rising sea levels caused by global warming. To protect our beaches, it is important to understand the process of how they change.

- **Put 3 to 4 inches of sand in one end of your tub to simulate a beach.** Add a couple inches of water in the other end.

- **Use a ruler or your hands to create waves to push the water in different directions.** Draw a diagram of what your beach looks like after each type of wave action.

- **Put the small blocks of wood along your beach shore to simulate buildings.** Repeat the wave patterns and note the results in your notebook.

- **Add water to your "ocean" in small amounts to simulate rising sea levels.** Note the changes to the shoreline.

- **Put the large block of wood in the water in front of a section of beach to simulate a sea wall.** What happens to the shoreline in front of that sea wall when you make strong wave movements? What happens to the shoreline further up the beach that is not protected by the sea wall?

To investigate more, research different solutions for preventing erosion and flooding of coastal communities. How are different cities and countries addressing this problem? Are there international efforts to protect the world's coastlines? How do individual efforts to protect private homes from coastal flooding affect the erosion of public beaches?

VOCAB LAB

Write down what you think each word means:

globalization, desertification, carbon marketplace, developing country, developed country, and **accretion.**

Compare your definitions with those of your friends or classmates. Did you all come up with the same meanings? Turn to the text and glossary if you need help.

Ideas for Supplies ▼

- a group of friends or classmates
- a collection of photographs of different categories of people

IDENTITY CRISIS

Race, gender, sexual orientation, age, nationality, religion, and ethnicity are some of the ways we identify ourselves. The tendency to categorize people by the groups they belong to means that we often see people from different groups in negative ways because we assume things about them without knowing them as individuals.

STEREOTYPES

All human beings have a basic psychological need to belong to a group. It gives us a sense of connectedness and security. But assigning specific traits to a person based on the group he belongs to is called stereotyping. What stereotypes do you have? How does it feel when other people stereotype you?

- **Show the pictures to each friend or classmate one at a time.** Ask each person to tell you what they think they know about this person based on the picture.

- **Record the responses on a chart that's divided into positive and negative responses.** As a group, discuss which responses were stereotypes.

- **Research why people stereotype.** What goes on in the human brain to make us want to categorize people? How can stereotypes be damaging to human relationships? What does research show is the best way to avoid automatically stereotyping people?

> To investigate more, go to a communal space such as a mall or a park. Dress in something very informal—jeans with holes, baseball cap, a T-shirt. Ask someone for the time. Record the person's verbal and nonverbal reaction. Repeat the experiment dressed another way, such as very formally. Do people react differently? What does this exercise tell you about stereotyping based on dress?

Aborigine: a descendent of the earliest inhabitants of Australia.

accretion: the gradual accumulation of layers of sediment.

adapt: to change one's behavior to fit into a new environment.

adorn: to decorate something.

alien: a person who has come from another country.

amnesty: when a government grants pardon to individuals for a law they have broken.

ancestor: a person from whom one is descended, such as a great-great-grandmother.

anthropology: the science of the physical and cultural origins of humans.

anti-Semitic: a person who is prejudiced or hostile toward Jewish people.

archaeologist: a scientist who specializes in the study of prehistoric cultures by analyzing artifacts and monuments.

Archimedes' principle: the physical law that a body immersed in a fluid is held up by a force equal to the weight of the fluid its body displaces.

artifact: an object made by humans for a purpose.

assimilation: to integrate people, ideas, and customs into a society.

association: when objects or ideas are connected in some way.

asylum: a protected status that governments can grant to immigrants fleeing a dangerous situation in their own country.

BCE: put after a date, BCE stands for Before Common Era and counts down to zero. CE stands for Common Era and counts up from zero. These nonreligious terms correspond to BC and AD. This book was printed in 2016 CE.

Beringia: the land between Siberia and Alaska that was exposed during the last Ice Age.

bipedalism: upright walking.

birth rate: the number of live births for every thousand people per year.

braceros: Mexican laborers allowed into the United States to work for a limited period of time as seasonal agricultural workers.

cannibal: someone who eats the flesh of another human being.

carbon dating: a scientific way of finding the age of organic material by measuring the amount of certain forms of carbon in the material.

carbon marketplace: a market created to encourage companies to lower their carbon dioxide emissions. The government places a limit on emissions, and companies that want to exceed this limit must purchase permits to do so. Companies that do not exceed their carbon dioxide limit can sell their extra allotment.

chromosome: a strand of DNA that is encoded with genetic material.

chronological: arranged in order of time.

citizenship: membership in a country.

civilization: a complex form of culture that includes cities, specialized workers, government and religious institutions, and advanced technology.

clan: a group of interrelated families.

classification: to systematically arrange items into groups based on common features these items have.

climate: the average weather patterns in an area during a long period of time.

climate change: changes in the earth's climate patterns, including rising temperatures, which is called global warming.

Clovis: a pre-historic Indian culture of North America characterized by technology with a distinctive stone projectile.

collaboration: working with others.

colonize: to settle an area.

communist: a system in which the government controls the economic resources of a nation.

community: a group of people who live in the same place or who share key characteristics such as religion or language.

conflict: disagreements which can be verbal or physical.

conquest: when one group conquers another.

conquistador: a Spanish conqueror of the sixteenth century.

controversy: a public disagreement between two sides.

convert: to change religion.

coprolite: fossilized feces.

cremation: to dispose of a dead person's body by burning it.

culture: the beliefs and way of life of a group of people, which can include religion, language, art, clothing, food, holidays, and more.

GLOSSARY

deoxyribonucleic acid (DNA): the molecule in all living things that carries genetic information.

deport: to expel a foreigner from a country.

desertification: the process by which fertile land becomes desert.

developed country: a country with an economy based on manufacturing and technology.

developing country: a poor agricultural country that is trying to develop industry.

diaspora: the spread of people outside their original homeland.

displaced: when people are forced to leave their home, usually because of war, persecution, or natural disaster.

domesticate: to tame animals through breeding.

drought: a prolonged period of abnormally low rainfall.

dwarfism: a genetic or medical condition that causes abnormally short stature.

dysentery: an infection of the intestines resulting in severe diarrhea.

economic depression: a slowdown in the economy accompanied by high unemployment and low wages.

emigrate: to leave one's own country in order to settle in another country.

empire: a large region controlled by one central government.

environmental: relating to the natural world and the impact of human activity on its condition.

erosion: the gradual wearing away of rock and soil by water and wind.

ethnic cleansing: the mass expulsion or killing of an unwanted group.

ethnic: sharing customs, languages, and beliefs.

evolution: the process by which a species changes over generations due to mutation and natural selection.

excavate: to dig up or uncover something.

extinct: when a species completely dies out.

famine: when food is extremely scarce and people face starvation.

Fertile Crescent: in ancient times, referred to a semi-circle of land stretching from the Nile River to the Persian Gulf.

fertile: rich soil that is capable of producing abundant crops.

fertility: able to produce or reproduce.

forced migration: when people are displaced from their homes because of war, persecution, or natural disaster.

forge: to shape metal into a tool by heating it up and hammering it into shape.

fossil: the preserved remains of a prehistoric plant or animal.

genetic marker: a recognizable gene that is inherited and can be used to trace family ancestry.

geneticist: a biologist who studies heredity.

genocide: destroying a racial, political, or cultural group or the language, religion, or culture of a group.

genome: an organism's complete set of genetic material.

genus: a subdivision of a family of organisms.

geologist: a scientist who studies the history of the earth through rock formations.

ghetto: a section of a city inhabited by one minority group.

globalization: the integration of the world economy through trade, money, and labor.

GPS: the abbreviation for Global Positioning System, a navigational system. This system uses satellites that allow people with receivers to determine their location anywhere in the world.

heredity: the passing of traits from one generation to another.

heritage: something that is passed from one generation to the next.

Holocaust: the killing of millions of Jews and other classes of people by the Nazis during World War II.

hominin: a group of primates that includes recent humans together with extinct ancestral and related forms.

Homo erectus: An extinct hominin species that lived in Africa and Eurasia between 1.9 million and 100,000 years ago. It is the oldest human to possess modern human-like body proportions.

Homo florensis: an extinct hominin species of dwarf stature that lived on the Indonesian island of Flores between 95,000 and 17,000 years ago.

Homo heidelbergensis: an extinct hominin species that lived in Africa, Europe, and possibly Asia between 700,000 and 200,000 years ago. It was the first species to routinely hunt large animals and build shelters.

Homo neanderthalensis: an extinct hominin species that lived in Europe and Southwest Asia between 400,000 and 28,000 years ago. This species is considered to be the closest relative to *Homo sapiens*.

Homo sapiens: the name of the genus and species of modern humans.

host: the country that receives immigrants.

husbandry: the care and cultivation of crops and animals.

hybrid: a person influenced by two different cultural backgrounds or an offspring of two different species.

hypothesis: a scientific theory tested through study and experimentation.

immigrant: a person who comes into a country to live permanently.

immigrate: to come into another country to live permanently.

immunity: a natural resistance to certain diseases.

incremental: slowly but steady.

indentured servant: a person bound by contract to work for another person for a defined period. Usually the servant does not receive pay but is given free passage to another country and room and board.

inscribe: to write or carve words or symbols on a document or object.

interbreeding: when one species mates with another species and produces offspring.

intolerance: the unwillingness to accept beliefs and behaviors different from one's own.

isolation: living separate from others.

isotopes: variations of the same kind of atom. Isotopes of an atom have the same number of protons but different numbers of neutrons.

Judaism: the religion developed by ancient Hebrews who believed in one god.

keel: a ridge that runs the length of a boat's hull.

kelp: seaweed.

kinetic energy: the energy a body gets from being in motion.

kosher: food that has been prepared according to Jewish religious law.

latitude: the distance of a place north or south of the equator.

lineage: the descendants of a common ancestor.

linguist: an expert in the study of languages.

logical: based on clear and sound reasoning.

longitude: the distance of a place east or west of the prime meridian, an imaginary line that runs from the North Pole to the South Pole.

megacity: a city with a population of more than 10 million.

midden: a deposit of trash.

migrant: someone who moves from place to place, usually to find work.

migrate: to move from one place to another.

migration: the movement of people to a new area or new country.

millennia: a period of a thousand years.

molecule: two or more atoms that are chemically bonded. Atoms are very small pieces of matter that make up everything in the universe.

monastery: a community of monks bound by religious vows.

monotheism: belief in one god.

mutation: a change in a gene or chromosome.

nomadic: without a permanent home.

nucleotides: a group of molecules that, when linked together, form the building blocks of DNA.

occipital bun: a bulge in the occipital bone at the back of the skull.

ocher: a pigment found in the earth.

opposable thumb: a thumb that can be used to grasp objects. This feature distinguishes primates from other mammals.

organism: any living thing, such as a plant or animal.

paleoanthropologist: a scientist who studies the fossilized remains of prehistoric humans.

peat: a brown, soil-like material found in bogs.

persecution: to treat people cruelly or unfairly because of their membership in a social, racial, ethnic, or political group.

plunder: to steal goods by force, usually in a time of war.

pogrom: an organized massacre of a particular group.

polytheistic: believing in more than one god.

poverty: having little money or material possessions.

prehistoric: the time before there were written records.

GLOSSARY

primate: a mammal that belongs to a classification order that shares the following features: large brain, opposable thumbs, good eyesight, and flexible toes.

primitive: being less developed.

proportional: corresponding in size.

prosper: to do well.

racism: to believe that all members of a race possess certain traits and to judge these traits as inferior to one's own. Negative opinions or treatment of people based on race.

Rastafari: a religious movement that originated in Jamaica. Followers believe that Africa is the promised land.

refuge: a place that gives protection.

refugee: someone escaping war, persecution, or natural disaster.

regime: the government in power.

resources: something a country has that supports its wealth, such as oil, water, food, money, and land.

revolution: a sudden and important change.

ritual: an established ceremony.

sacred: holy.

sanctuary: a place of refuge or safety.

savannah: grassland.

Scandinavia: the region of northern Europe that includes Denmark, Norway, Sweden, and Finland.

scant: a very limited amount.

scapegoat: a person or group who must bear the blame for others.

scientific method: the way scientists ask questions and do experiments to try to prove their ideas.

scurvy: a disease caused by a diet lacking in vitamin C.

sediment: bits of rock, sand, or dirt that have been carried to a place by water and wind.

segregate: to require people to live separately from the main group in society.

slum: a heavily populated, run-down section of a city.

society: an organized community of people with shared laws, traditions, and values.

sojourn: a temporary stay.

species: a group of organisms that share common traits and can reproduce offspring of their own kind.

speculate: to form a theory without solid evidence.

stereotype: the inaccurate belief that all people who share a single physical or cultural trait are the same.

sustenance: something that keeps a person alive.

symbolic behavior: when people in a culture develop meanings for items or behaviors that represent something different than what that item or behavior appears to be.

synagogue: a building used for Jewish religious services.

technology: tools, methods, and systems used to solve a problem or do work.

temperate: the moderate climate zones between the tropical and polar regions.

tenant farmer: a person who farms rented land.

trafficker: a person who buys or sells illegal goods, or illegally moves people.

trait: a feature or quality that makes somebody or something recognizable.

uniformitarianism: the theory that processes that can be observed in the world today happened in the past with the same results, which means that the present is key to understanding the past. While this theory originated to explain geological processes, scientists in other disciplines use it as well.

urban: relating to a city.

Viking: Seafaring pirates and traders from Scandinavia who migrated throughout Europe in the eighth to eleventh centuries.

RESOURCES

BOOKS

Atlas of Human Migration, Russell King, Firefly, 2007.

Changing Planet: What Is the Environmental Impact of Human Migration and Settlement?, Sally Morgan, Crabtree Publishing Company, 2010.

Kids Like Me: Voices of the Immigrant Experience, Judith M. Blohm and Terri Lapinsky, Intercultural, 2006.

Migration in the 21st Century: How Will Globalization and Climate Change Affect Migration and Settlement?, Paul Challen, Crabtree Publishing Company, 2010.

Pushes & Pulls: Why Do People Migrate?, Robert Walker, Crabtree Publishing Company, 2010.

Their Skeletons Speak: Kennewick Man and the Paleoamerican World, Sally M. Walker and Douglas W. Owsley, Carolrhoda, 2012.

Walking the Earth: The History of Human Migration, Tricia Andryszewski, Twenty-First Century, 2006.

WEBSITES

National Geographic Genographic Project: The Human Journey: Migration Routes
genographic.nationalgeographic.com/human-journey

American Anthropological Association Race—Are We So Different?
understandingrace.org/home.html

Smithsonian National Museum of Natural History What Does It Mean to be Human?
humanorigins.si.edu/evidence/human-family-tree

Modern Faces Give Clues to Ancient Migration
abroadintheyard.com/modern-faces-ancient-migration

QR CODE GLOSSARY

Page 6: outofedenwalk.nationalgeographic.com

Page 16: channel.nationalgeographic.com/diggers/videos/diggers-blog-archaeologists-tools

Page 21: understandingrace.org/home.html

Page 27: www.le.ac.uk/richardiii/multimedia/videos/ct-scan.html

Page 43: linkengpark.com/incredible-human-journey-2009-part-1-3

Page 44: jawoyn.org

Page 48: smithsonianmag.com/travel/prehistoric-rock-art-visit-around-world-180952989/?no-ist

Page 56: lascaux.culture.fr/#/fr/00.xml

Page 58: pbs.org/wgbh/nova/ancient/explore-pre-clovis-sites.html

Page 71: youtube.com/watch?v=W6WO5XabD-s

Page 72: sagadb.org

Page 77: nationalhumanitiescenter.org/pds/amerbegin/settlement/text1/JamestownPercyObservations.pdf

Page 86: inmotionaame.org/migrations/landing.cfm;jsessionid=f8302412081448029771603?migration=8&bhcp=1

Page 88: lens.blogs.nytimes.com/2015/06/04/rohingya-refugees-stateless-in-southeast-asia/?_r=2

Page 90: nytimes.com/interactive/2014/08/13/upshot/where-people-in-each-state-were-born.html

Page 91: libertyellisfoundation.org/passenger-result

Page 93: amhistory.si.edu/onthemove/themes/story_51_5.html

Page 94: poeticwaves.net

Page 96: slavevoyages.org

Page 99: cloudchasersgame.com

Page 104: mckinsey.com/insights/economic_studies/global_cities_of_the_future_an_interactive_map

INDEX

INDEX